SECOND EDITION

A FEW FOOTPRINTS

By J. PASSMORE EDWARDS

(From the painting by G. F. Watts, R.A., by kind permission of Mrs. Watts)

London:

WATTS & CO.,

17, JOHNSON'S COURT, FLEET STREET, E.C.

Copies of this Publication may be had in cloth, price One Shilling each

A FEW FOOTPRINTS

BY

J. PASSMORE EDWARDS

" Do the best for the most "

LONDON :
WATTS & CO.,
17, JOHNSON'S COURT, FLEET STREET, E.C.
1906

The first edition of this booklet was printed in August, 1905, not for sale, but for private circulation, and for the reasons mentioned in the Introductory paragraph. Since then an unexpected demand has arisen for it, and the present edition, with some additional facts and comments, is provided to meet such demand.

A FEW FOOTPRINTS

INTRODUCTORY

I HAVE again and again been asked by publishers and literary interviewers to write a biographical sketch of myself, or to supply, or assist in supplying, the necessary materials for the purpose; but I have always declined, because I thought that anything I may have said or done was scarcely entitled to such specific notice; and also because I had not finished the educational and ameliorative work I had marked out for myself. Many sketches and accounts, however, of one kind or another, have, from time to time, been published in magazines or newspapers without my concurrence or consent; and all of them, as far as I know, have been more or less inaccurate. For instance, one account, recently published in book form, and consisting of 160 pages, says:—"In the year 1889 the Rev. C. F. Mythian, Vicar of Blackwater, and president of its little Institute, wrote Mr. Passmore Edwards asking his assistance in the shape of books." The author should have said, if he said anything, "The Rev. C. F. Rogers, Vicar of Mythian," as Blackwater, my birthplace, is only a small village in the parish of Mythian. Referring to my first engagement on the Press, the author says: "He obtained a post on the *Citizen* paper, published in Manchester." He should have said the *Sentinel* newspaper, published in London. Another writer in another publication says I "bought *The Builder* from Mr. George Maddick." He should have said, if he said anything, that I bought *The Building News* from Messrs. Kelly. I ought perhaps to share the blame for the publication of such inaccuracies, as I have declined opportunities offered me to supply data and correct proofs. Unfortunately, these and other mistakes have been reproduced in other publications; and to prevent, if possible, their recurrence, and in the interest of fact and self-protection, I have jotted down the following fragmentary reminiscences.

EARLY DAYS.

I WAS born March 24th, 1823, in Blackwater, a small village, situated between Redruth and Truro, in Cornwall, which contained at the time about two hundred inhabitants. My father was a Cornishman and by trade a carpenter, and my mother, whose maiden name was Passmore, was a native of Newton Abbot, Devonshire. I had three brothers, William, Richard, and James. The cottage in which I and my brothers were born consisted of four small rooms. As there was not much carpentering to do in the neighbourhood, and my father not being fully employed, he built, mainly by borrowed money, a larger house near by, for which he obtained a public-house licence. Though the new house had eight small rooms, it had more rooms than windows ; consequently two bedrooms at the back of the house had no direct window light, but only borrowed light from a small window between the two rooms, over the stairs. I mention this circumstance to recall the fact that during the early part of the last century almost everything consumed by the people was taxed, including the wood, glass, and other materials used in the production of windows, *and the windows as well*. One of the results of this state of things was that I, with one of my brothers, slept thousands of times in a small bedroom into which the light of heaven never directly entered. As with us, so with hundreds of thousands of others. The window tax alone assisted to enfeeble the British race. As with the window tax, so with hundreds of other taxes, including the tax on bread, which still more enfeebled the race, and which a partisan statesmanship would triumphantly re-impose, and thereby endanger the power and prosperity of the country. I well remember some of the blighting effects of the Corn Laws, when large numbers of the industrious poor of Cornwall ate barley bread, and many had not enough of that. The repeal of the Corn Laws and the introduction of a Free Trade era soon broadened and brightened national prospects.

My father not only brewed his own beer, which he sold " on the premises," but he supplied beer to some of the beershops in the adjacent villages. A copper mine, however, having been started near by, or rather an old mine having been revived, drained away the water from our pump ; and the little brewing business gradually dried up, the little public-house business having dried up several years before. My father then cultivated a large garden, which surrounded the house, and which was most productive, particularly of strawberries. These, when gathered, were sent for sale to neighbouring towns on market days. I, for years after I left school, assisted in brewing, in gardening, and in carrying strawberries to market.[1]

My only school education was obtained at the village school, which was conducted by Mr. James Blackney, who became schoolmaster after he had injured his health by working underground as a miner. He commenced his school and carried it on for a year or two in a room about nine feet square, and afterwards in a little schoolroom built for the purpose. He taught reading, writing, and arithmetic, and a smattering of grammar and geography; and once a week he treated his scholars with a good dose of catechism, when he read both questions and answers. One of the questions I thought at the time, and all the time I was at school, was "Who are water devils?" and, when hearing it, I imagined fiery devils plunging about in water. The question in reality was "Who and what are devils?" I give this as a specimen of the quality of the teaching we received. Mr. Blackney was, nevertheless, a painstaking and conscientious man, and he has always had a green spot in my memory. His general teaching fee was twopence a week, and threepence a week for older and more advanced scholars. I remember one evening, after school hours, his calling on my father and saying that the time had come to increase his school fee for me from twopence to threepence weekly. My father at first demurred to the increased claim, but when told I was making good progress consented, and I for a year or two longer remained a day scholar, and afterwards for twelve or fifteen months as an evening scholar at twopence a week.

When I was about ten years of age a cholera wave passed over the country, and additional sanitary arrangements were demanded; and my father was appointed one of two inspectors to see that they were complied with in our village. At that time most of the cottages, with their immediate surroundings, were in a most

---

[1] When opening the Redruth Free Library in May, 1895, I said: "Many a time I walked the three miles from Blackwater to Redruth, under a June or July sun, with three or four gallons of strawberries, and, after selling them as I best could, returned home with a light heart in proportion to the money value I received. Had I anticipated or dreamed then that nearly half a century after I should bring to Redruth something very different from and more lasting than strawberries—a public library—and that I should receive such smiles and good wishes as had been showered upon me that day, I should have walked home with less anxiety and a more elastic heart."

insanitary condition. The wonder was, and is, that during the early part of the last century contagious diseases were not more numerous and destructive than they were. In consequence of improved regulations both cholera and small-pox, which paid periodic visits to the district, became less and less. The two evils, fed and fostered by the same causes, were resisted and driven back by the same means. But, while improved sanitation in Cornwall and throughout the country has had the credit for reducing or banishing cholera, a similar diminution of small-pox has been attributed to vaccination !

About this time my brother William, who was four years my senior, suffered so much from indigestion that the doctor of the district had to be consulted, and he, like most other members of the profession at the time, advised that my brother should be bled. This was done, and I was appointed to hold the basin to receive the blood. When the basin was about half full a giddiness came over me, and I fainted and fell to the ground. How long I was unconscious I cannot say, but when I revived I found myself in a chair in the open air with water trickling over me. Being a strong lad, I soon got over my mishap. Not so my brother. He did not faint or suffer less from indigestion, but he got, and remained, weaker for some time ; and for many years after, at the same time of the year, he felt languid and depressed ; and there is reason to believe that bleeding impaired rather than improved his health, and perhaps shortened his life. When bled, he wanted not less, but more or better blood, which might have been obtained by change of diet or exercise or air at the seaside. Bleeding then, and for centuries before, and many years after, was generally considered and acted on by medical men as a panacea for most ills ; and many generations of many nations have had to suffer, and still suffer, in consequence. No one can tell, or will ever be able to tell, the extent of the injury inflicted on mankind by prevalent phlebotomy from the time of Pascal to that of Lord Byron, and from the time of Byron to that of Count Cavour, the last recorded illustrious victim of the practice. Proof of the high estimate put upon it may be seen in the fact that the chief organ of the medical profession in this country has been for generations, and is to this day, called the *Lancet*.

Pursuit of Knowledge under Difficulties.

When I was about twelve years of age, the only London periodical that came into the village was the *Penny Magazine*, published by Charles Knight, and that was taken in by my father. I well remember the number that contained a bio-graphical sketch with portrait of John Hunter. The article began somewhat in this way :—" John Hunter, the greatest anatomist of modern times." I asked my mother the meaning of the word " anatomist," and she told me to consult the dictionary. I did so, and got a little wiser. I had to go to the same source to know the meaning of the word " modern." I read on and on, with the dictionary as tutor, and got sufficiently interested in the subject to feel boyish flutterings of ambition to become known and useful in some way myself. From that time—1835—to the present—1905— I have nurtured a similar desire, which time does not wither nor changing circumstances modify.

Books in my father's house were few, and fewer still in most of the houses in the village ; and the books within reach were more theological than interesting. When I got a year or two older, and managed, by putting pennies together, to save a shilling or two, I occasionally walked from Blackwater to Truro—six miles—to buy, at a second-hand bookshop, the best, or what I thought the best, books my slender means would allow. Having read of Locke and Newton as great names linked in fame, I resolved to buy and read their works. The first I managed to pick up was a second-hand copy of Newton's *Optics*, which I read as I best could, and was just as wise at the end as I was at the beginning of reading it. I was more fascinated with the fine title, Locke's *Essay on the Human Understanding*. This I could not get at second hand, and had to order it through the old pensioner who supplied the *Penny Magazine*. After reading Locke's *Essay* I found myself almost as much at sea as when trying to follow Newton in analysing sunlight. This double disenchantment assisted to chasten my zeal in the pursuit of knowledge, and to limit my reading to humbler themes.

My father rather discouraged than encouraged reading, and particularly in the daytime. On winter evenings the room in which the family mostly lived was lighted by a single candle, similar to what miners used underground. Such candles in those days required frequent snuffing, but they rarely got it. I, however, by aid of such light, managed to read while others were talking or moving about ; and hundreds and hundreds of times I pressed my thumbs firmly on my ears until they ached, in order to read with as little distraction as possible. In this way I managed fre-quently to entertain myself and pick up fragments of knowledge. These recollections of early days, fresh and vivid as those of yesterday, have encouraged me in after years to promote the public library movement, so that poor boys and girls, as well as men and women, may enjoy educational or recreative advantages denied to many during the early and middle parts of the last century. I have in several instances, when building public libraries, provided reading-rooms for the special use of boys.

At school there was only one room for boys and girls, and I fell deeply in love with a schoolgirl. There was no doubt about it. For a year or two before I left school, and a year or two after, she was " the goddess of my idolatry." In consequence of helping her mother at home, she generally came to school late, and I was much more interested in watching the door to see her enter than attending to my lessons. I wrote her love-letters, some of which she received, and others were never sent, because I stood in fear of her big brother, who threatened to thrash me if I wrote to his sister. Sometimes I picked the best and largest strawberries I could find in my father's garden, folded them neatly in cabbage-leaves, and walked round her father's house at evening times in the hope of seeing her ; and when I did, and was sufficiently fortunate to give her the strawberries, I went home more in love than ever. But I made little or no impression, and for a good reason : she was a year and a half older than I was, and loved another who was about a year and a half older than she was. I nevertheless did my best, and made the most of myself to win favour. On Sundays I took little stones in my pocket to chapel, and put them under the heels of my shoes when I stood up to make myself look taller. I also made myself a young, cunning, and not very scrupulous diplomatist, and used all the means within reach, or that I was capable of inventing, to sow suspicion and produce dissension between my adored one and my rival. But I made no progress, and the result was my unrequited affection gradually decayed, and left me none the worse for the consuming ordeal through which I passed.

On love, on grief, on every human thing,
Time sprinkles Lethe-waters with his wing.

MOTHER AND FATHER.

My mother was a Baptist, and my father, though not a Baptist, was a Calvinist in belief. He frequently went on Sunday mornings, taking one or two of his boys with him, to the Baptist chapel, about a mile off, and to the Wesleyan chapel in the village on Sunday afternoons. He was prone to criticise, in a hostile spirit, the sermons delivered at the Wesleyan chapel. He abjured Wesley as much as he admired Toplady, and balanced his depreciation of Arminianism by his appreciation of Calvinism. Though I heard, when a boy, several hundred sermons, I do not remember a single passage or anecdote given in any one of them. I well remember, however, how sleepy I frequently got at the afternoon services, and the scores of times I pinched myself or pulled my hair to prevent nodding or falling from the form. We all sat on forms without backs in Cornish village chapels in those days. I also well remember how eagerly I anticipated the perorations of a Wesleyan travelling minister (Christopher by name), when he described in glowing language the joys of the redeemed and the tortures of the damned. When he preached, and particularly at the end of his sermons, I was wide awake. I then listened with rapt attention, or as if I were witnessing the closing scene of a tragic performance on the stage. His florid descriptions so arrested and swayed my imagination that in my dreams I occasionally awoke in fright on seeing the world on fire, accompanied by scenes that might have given Dante excruciating suggestions for his *Inferno*. I mention these things not to undervalue preaching to young people, but to suggest that such preaching, to be beneficial, should be adapted to the youthful mind.

My mother rarely went to chapel. Her household duties and anxieties were as numerous and as necessary on Sundays as on other days. She put her religion into her life. She said little and did much. She quietly and without a murmur did the many things she had to do from day to day, and from hour to hour. The cares and claims of home bounded her ambition and fully occupied her thoughts and hands. She was essentially a peacemaker. I never knew her to cause a family jar, or to say a word against a neighbour, or to give offence to anyone. Blessed be her name and memory! I sometimes think that, could she, when absorbed in work and anxiety, have glanced in fancy into the future, and seen how, fifty, sixty, or seventy years after, she would be so loved and reverenced, an additional smile might now and then have brightened her serious face. But perhaps it is better as it was and is. She did her best from a sense of duty and for the love of it, without a thought or expectation that for so doing her memory would be embalmed in the memory of others. She rests from her labours. She died in my brother Richard's house at Bath in May, 1870, soon after she had entered on the eighty-sixth year of her age. I have been privileged to dedicate to her memory the Cornwall Convalescent Home at Perranporth, the Public Library at Newton

Abbot,[1] where she was born, and one of the Homes at the Colony for the benefit of Epileptics at Chalfont, Buckinghamshire.

OLD HALES.

During my early school-boy days there lived in Blackwater, with his wife and children, in a miserable, tumble-down house, a man who was known as "Old Hales." Many years before he was sent to prison for larceny, and from that time he lost his character, and was treated as an enemy of society. He lived, if it could be called living, by cadging of one kind or another, and by doing odd jobs, when he could get them to do, for very little pay. If hen-roosts were invaded, or ducks and geese were missing, "Old Hales" would have the discredit of having removed them, whether he deserved it or not. He was, however, not so bad as he was painted. For instance, hearing that my father wanted some stones to build a garden hedge, "Old Hales" offered to get some, which would be got only at the expense of very hard work, great difficulty and danger. At that time, when a shaft for mining was sunk, its mouth, or the part near the surface, for twelve or fifteen feet, was faced round with large stones closely arranged and well mortared together. "Old Hales" offered, at the imminent risk of life and limb, to get from the shafts of a used-up mine near by several cartloads of stones so placed, for insignificant pay. By so doing, an insecure step or blow, or a momentary loss of balance, might end in a fall of hundreds of fathoms, and certain death. My father discouraged the undertaking; but "Old Hales," with heroic fortitude, commenced and completed the work, and did for a few shillings what ninety-nine working-men out of a hundred would not, or could not, do, as he did it, for a hundred times the pay. By so doing he not only showed ability and willingness to work, but high qualities of head, heart, and hand. Not long after he was again arrested for stealing, found guilty, and sentenced to be transported for life to Botany Bay, and was never heard of again. He deserved a better fate, and had fortune during his earlier years been more favourable he might, and probably would, have become a law-abiding and useful, if not a leading, member of our village society. Poor "Old Hales"!

[1] When my mother was about ten years of age her father, who was by trade a saddler, removed with his family from Newton Abbot to Exeter, where they lived for many years in a corner house, one part of which faced one street and another part faced a side street. My grandfather kept a parrot, which was sometimes hung in his cage on one side of the house and at other times on the other side. But wherever he was he would repeat in plain language "Passmore-Saddler-round-the-corner," and in this way acted as a cheap and characteristic advertisement.

SOME TRIAL TRIPS.

I have forgotten many things, but not my first appearance in public. It was a notable day—the day when Queen Victoria was crowned. Blackwater and one or two of the adjoining villages rejoiced in possessing between them a musical band, of which I was the youngest member, and in which I played the fife. Unusual preparations were made in Redruth, the largest town in the district, to celebrate the Coronation, and our little band offered its services to join in the festivities. The offer was accepted. I, in order to attract undue attention, and to astonish the boys, played too loudly, and the leader of the band, who played the trombone, said more than once during the day: "Jack Edwards,[1] you play out of tune." I have since had occasion to remember the admonition then given me, and have found that my capacity for getting out of tune survived from the day of the Coronation of Queen Victoria in 1838 to that of the Coronation of Edward VII. in 1902, and after. When I have made mistakes which might have been avoided, or undertaken to do something for which I was unfitted, or more than I was able to accomplish, or thought more of the passing moment than the superior claims of the future, or more of fleeting than enduring interests, an inner voice has whispered: "You are out of tune." It is easy to get out of tune and to stay there, and the best way to get into tune and stay there is to do the best for the most, and then our respective life notes will harmonise with the music of the spheres.

When about fifteen years old I gave evidence that my ambition outstripped my ability. I tried my hand at poetry, and sent some verses which I thought good to the *West Briton* for insertion in its "Poet's Corner," and was chagrined a few days after to see under "Answers to Correspondents" that my "Song of the Rose" was "not worth the space it would occupy, if any space at all." This assisted to damp, if not to extinguish, my poetic aspirations. A year or two after I tried lecturing, with a little more success. I frequently attended the meetings of a Literary Society at Carharrack, about three miles from Blackwater, and actually offered to give a lecture to men most of whom were old enough to be my father. Strange to say, my offer was accepted, and still stranger

---

[1] *Chart and Compass*, the organ of the British and Foreign Sailors' Society, thinks it is an interesting coincidence that "Jack" Edwards, the Cornish boy, should in after years become the founder of "Jack's Palace" in Commercial Road, Stepney.

when I mention the subject, "The Poetry of Creation." I knew precious little about poetry, and less about creation. At the appointed time I read my lecture, and could only have given myself satisfaction, as I neither provoked laughter nor won applause, neither got a vote of censure nor a vote of thanks.

My next attempt was a complete failure. I offered—and the offer was accepted—to speak at the annual meeting of the Young Men's Association at St. Agnes. I made, as I thought, ample preparation. The speech was not to be read, like the lecture, but reeled off from memory, where I supposed it was firmly fixed. When called on, I began confidently enough, but had not gone far when I tripped over a sentence or two, got confused, and, after two or three unsuccessful attempts to pick up the threads of my speech, I had to sit down, amid scornful laughter. Not liking to be beaten, and remembering, as I thought, the other parts of the speech, I made another attempt, which soon ended in another failure, when I again had to sit down, and was saluted with another and louder peal of laughter. To increase my discomfiture, the chairman, who was a bit of a wag, related an anecdote. He said some years before a clergyman in a neighbouring parish had one day, when preaching, to leave the pulpit to part two fighting dogs, one of them being his own, outside the church. During his absence the wind blew a portion of his written sermon out of the window near by. When he returned he looked at his MS., and, not finding the part he expected, said: "Where was I last?" "Parting the dogs, sir," said a boy in the congregation. "But I thought I had come to 'thirdly,'" said the clergyman. "'Thirdly' is gone out of the window," replied the boy. "And so it is with Mr. Edwards," said the chairman. "His 'secondly' and 'thirdly' have vanished into space." More loud laughter, in which all joined but the would-be orator, who that evening returned home a sadder and wiser youth.

I was more successful in another enterprise. My education, though so very limited, was superior to that of many others in the district, some of whom had no education at all. When I was about seventeen years of age, with the cordial assistance of my much-respected friend and schoolfellow John Symons, and the encouragement of a few villagers, we commenced a free evening and Sunday morning school to teach uneducated men and boys. This was done on two week-day evenings and on Sunday mornings in a little "Brianite" chapel near by. Writing-tables were made and erected round the chapel by voluntary labour. During school-time these tables were raised and sustained on supports. For religious services the supports, being movable, were taken away, and the tables, suspended on hinges, descended close to the wall. In this way the little chapel answered the double purpose of a school and a chapel. At first we encountered opposition from some people, who thought that writing and ciphering were too secular to be taught on Sundays. The opposition, however, soon subsided in the presence of many improved and grateful pupils. The school did useful work for years. Though it has since been my privilege to commence in other parts much larger educational enterprises, I cherish no rosier recollections than those which cluster around that little village Sunday morning and week-day evening school; and few letters in after life have given me more satisfaction than three or four I have received from men who there, as men or boys, learnt to read and write.

About this time—1842—I was not only an apprentice lecturer, but an amateur propagandist. A ripple of the agitation for the repeal of the Corn Laws reached Blackwater, and, hearing that the Anti-Corn Law League gratuitously supplied tracts and pamphlets, I wrote to Manchester and solicited a few for distribution. Three or four days after I received a letter from Mr. George Wilson, the Chairman of the League, thanking me for my proposed co-operation. Had I been a clergyman or a known local squire, I could not have expected or received a more cordial reply. A few days after I received a bulky parcel of Anti-Corn Law literature, forty times more than I expected, and all at once I secured more than village fame. Having freely received, I freely distributed. One day I happened to meet the son of the Mayor of Penzance, to whom I gave some tracts. Shortly after, being in Penzance on my self-appointed mission, I called on the young man at his father's house. After a little ceremonial delay I was ushered into the presence, not of the young man, but of his father—Mr. Samuel Bidwell—the Mayor himself, who, assuming a judge-like attitude, and looking at me severely, said: " Do you know, young man, that I am a magistrate, and have the power to send you to prison for sedition?" A little frightened, and fearing I had done something wrong, I asked in somewhat subdued terms : " What for?" " What for, sir? Because you have given my son, and distributed in the neighbourhood, seditious tracts on the Corn Laws, and if you do so again to him or to anyone else in this town I will have you arrested and sent to prison. Be off now, and don't let me see your face or hear of you again, or it will be the worse for you." I was glad enough to leave the house, and mention the circumstance, not merely to revive a comical recollection, but to show the narrow, tyrannical spirit which animated some food-taxers sixty or more years ago. I was, however, neither crushed nor dismayed by the Mayor's mingled frown and threat, but went on my way distributing Free Trade literature as before, and am ready and willing now, two generations after, to repeat the offence.

SUMMER SUNSETS.

The country round about Blackwater was the reverse of picturesque, and was made more so by the many "knacked" or used-up mines which abounded, and which resembled so many small exhausted volcanoes. But what the district lacked in rural beauty was occasionally made up, and more than made up, by cloud scenery, and particularly by sunsets over the sea. Nature, with simple mixtures of light and vapour, produces an infinite variety of sky scenery. At times the clouds over the sea appeared like magnificent mountains bathed in amber or purple ; or rainbow-tinted valleys, threaded with silver streams ; or forests fringed with fire ; or glorified islands floating in an azure sea.

> Like a prairie
> Left upon the level water,
> One long track and trail of splendour.

Some people worship the rising sun. I should prefer to worship the setting sun, and particularly when he pours his joy-laden benedictions on Cornish coasts, and when I know he will leave behind him a flood of tender twilight, and so intimate with a pale dawn his rising over other lands and seas, and so on and on for ever.

One evening in later years, while admiring an unusually fine sunset over St. Ive's Bay, when sea and sky met in lustrous union, a man with a gun on his shoulder and a dog by his side passed, and I ventured to ask him whether they frequently witnessed such sights. He looked at me somewhat drowsily, and said : "I don't know ; I would rather see a good dog-fight." A step from the sublime to the ridiculous ! Here was a well-dressed, well-fed Englishman who preferred to see dogs mangle each other, or birds he had shot fall mutilated to the ground, than witness a scene worthy of a seraph's song. But this man, probably without knowing it, carried with him germs of moral ability which might, in favourable circumstances, blossom into beauty and yield more genuine joy than ever was, or ever will be, derived from blood-stained sports. The man and gun incident reminds me of another and different one. On an occasion when an English visitor was sauntering on and admiring a very fine sunset over some Welsh hills, he passed an elderly and poorly-clad woman sitting on a bank quietly enjoying the scene. He spoke to her about its peculiar colouring. After a short pause, she said, in reply: "Yes, some people like to talk about such splendour—I prefer to sit still and soak it in."[1]

IN A LAWYER'S OFFICE.

I was taught no trade, and consequently became anxious about my future. My father having some business to do with **Mr. H. S. Stokes**, a well-known lawyer in Truro, and hearing that he wanted an under clerk, made application on my behalf to fill the post; and to this, when between nineteen and twenty years of age, I was appointed, at £10 a year salary. After commencing my new duties, and while performing them, I walked every Monday morning from Blackwater to Truro, and carried my dinners—always Cornish pasties made by my mother—for the first three days of the week, and every Thursday she made and sent me three other pasties for the other three days of the week. Dining on cold pasties every week-day, and particularly when most of them were two or three days old, was not very appetising. I managed, however, with good bread and butter for my other meals, to enjoy good health. I went on in this way for eighteen months, when Mr. Stokes, finding, I suppose, that I was either unfit for the situation, or that he had not enough for me to do, told me that he should not require my services any longer; and so ended an uninteresting portion of my life. Mr. Stokes was then, and for fifty years after, much and deservedly respected as lawyer, literary man, and county official. As poet he earned more than local fame, as his correspondence with Longfellow, Tennyson, and others testified. He, however, never bestowed on me, while I was in his office, a single smile, or gave me a word of encouragement. But

---

[1] I said, when opening the Holiday Home for the Sunday-school Union at Clacton-on-Sea, in June, 1899: "There is more sunshine in the world than shadow. How can that be, someone may ask, when a half of the world is always in sunshine and the other half in shadow? That, however, is not so. Thanks to the refracting power of light when passing through air or water, the world every morning has a spell of twilight before the sun rises, and an equally consoling spell after the sun sets. It may be said that every part of the world has about twelve and a-half hours of sunlight, or what is equal to it, and about eleven and a-half hours without sunlight. Besides, while the sun is illuming and warming the other side of the world, we on this side have the stars smiling on us to encourage thought and nurture hope. There is, in fact, not only more sunshine than shadow, but more good than evil, more joy than sorrow, more life than death, and more victory than defeat in the world."

when, more than forty years after, I provided public buildings in Cornwall, he more than once, on public occasions, referred in complacent language to our former connection.

A RUN FOR LIFE.

While I was so engaged with Mr. Stokes, two brothers—Lightfoot by name—were executed at Bodmin for murdering Mr. Neville Norway, a well-known Cornishman, and I, like thousands of other foolish people from far and near, went to witness the public tragedy. After it was over I walked from Bodmin to Truro—twenty-two miles. Being alone nearly all the way, I had ample time to think well over the event of the day, and concluded, in my own way, that death punishments were more harmful than otherwise; that they placed criminals beyond the reach of repentance or reform; that publicly taking away human life in the presence of thousands of spectators did not teach the sanctity of life, but the contrary; that the doom of executed men was irrevocable; and if the voice of circumstances, as interpreted at the trial, did not reveal the truth, a huge mistake might have been made. When I had walked more than three-quarters of the journey, I overtook, in a somewhat lonely part of the road, two men who had also seen the execution. They accosted me, and after a little conversation had passed between us, not liking their appearance, and to leave them behind, I more than once quickened my pace, and they did the same. They, in fact, continued to force their attention on me, and, acting as if they understood each other, awoke in me a suspicion that they meant no good, and intended to rob me. I felt alarmed, and commenced running as fast as I could, and, to my horror, found they were following me with all their might. I, being younger, and a pretty good runner, gradually left them behind, and after running about a quarter of a mile they gave up the chase. I, though getting tired and footsore, continued to run for a mile or more. But I saw no more of the two men, who probably intended to rob me, and, if they did, rather than be found out they might have served me as the Lightfoots had served Mr. Neville Norway, and I should not be here to tell the tale.

FROM BLACKWATER TO MANCHESTER.

I had now to look about in earnest to do something for a living. I had certain literary aspirations, with only very little literary equipment. At last I summoned up sufficient courage to call on the editor of the *West Briton* in Truro, and offered him my services for anything he might consider they were worth. He listened kindly, but could promise nothing. When leaving the office I happened to meet Mr. R. K. Philp, who was travelling through the country in the interests of the *Sentinel*, a sixpenny weekly newspaper just started in London. There were no half-penny, penny, twopenny, or threepenny newspapers in those days in London. In the course of conversation Mr. Philp said he was instructed by his employers to appoint an agent for the paper in Manchester when he got there, and, hearing I had corresponded with the Chairman of the Anti-Corn Law League and made myself useful by distributing its literature, he thought, as I was in want of employment, I might represent the new paper in that town. I seized the proposal, and then and there undertook to go to Manchester and perform the necessary duties for £40 a year. So commenced an important change in my life. I returned to Blackwater with elastic steps and still more elastic hopes. But my joy for weeks was chequered with misgivings. Manchester was a long way off, and my intellectual and pecuniary means slender. Was I, without experience, equal to the duties I was expected to perform? Such thoughts, however, were swept aside by preparations for my venturesome journey from the West to the North—from my small native village to mighty Manchester.

How to get to Manchester was a matter of some importance. To go by railway and have enough to live on for a week or two would cost more than I could command. After full inquiry I decided to go from Falmouth to Dublin as steerage passenger for ten shillings, from Dublin to Liverpool for three shillings, and then to Manchester by rail for two shillings and sixpence. Shillings and sixpences had to be carefully guarded by me in those days. In due time I made ready for the eventful journey. My luggage was neatly and tenderly packed into a carpet-bag made for the occasion by my mother. It was made of stair carpet, and resembled a sack about two feet deep and eighteen inches in diameter. It was held together at the top by a brass chain, which passed through about a dozen small brass rings secured to the bag and fastened with a padlock. Into this were placed all my worldly possessions, and at last the parting day came, when, with overflowing emotion, I left home and friends to commence, in untried circumstances, an uncertain career. The passage from Falmouth to Dublin occupied forty-eight hours—forty-eight hours of misery. It was winter time; I was cold and ill nearly all the while, and had to pack myself away, as I best could, in the company of barrels, boxes, and luggage, under a large tarpaulin. It was not much better, but

C

happily much shorter, from Dublin to Liverpool, when my fellow passengers were half a hundred pigs, whose united screams, until we got out to sea, made a more hideous noise than was ever before heard on sea or land.

In Manchester.

As arranged, I met Mr. Philp in Manchester, and soon learned that the prospects of the *Sentinel* were not so rosy as I expected. I, however, commenced work with zeal, and a resolve to do my very best for the paper. I attended meetings, and sent short accounts of them to London. I distributed circulars and called on booksellers, newsagents, and others in their homes or offices, in the interests of the paper. I visited many of the towns in Lancashire and Cheshire on a similar errand, and always travelled in railway trucks, or exactly as cattle were taken from place to place. But I had great difficulty in getting pay from London, and had to borrow small sums from my friends in Cornwall; and even then I should have been stranded but for the kindness of Mr. James Hibbert and his sister, who kept a little shop in Bridge Street, and who, knowing my circumstances, allowed me to live with them month after month on credit. I received only ten pounds from the *Sentinel* for fifteen months' devoted service. The paper, in fact, was a commercial failure, and I had to pick up a living as I best could in some other direction. Being a teetotaler and a rather fluent talker, I offered my services as lecturer to temperance societies in the Manchester district, at a few shillings a lecture. In this way I managed to keep my head above water until the latter part of 1845, when, after a visit to my parents and friends in Cornwall, I came to London in the twenty-second year of my age, to try my fortunes on a wider sea.

Though I had a rather rough time in Manchester, I enjoyed while there some advantages, and among them was that of being a member of its Mechanics' Institute. I there heard several well-known men lecture, men who were popular at the time, but whose names now, "like streaks of morning cloud, are melting into the infinite azure of the past." Among them were Sheridan Knowles, Sir H. R. Bishop, Robert Haydon, Cowden Clarke, and Dr. Robert Vaughan. Mr. Hibbert, who spontaneously befriended me, lent me the works of Dr. Channing, which I first read with caution, and afterwards with delight. Reading Channing prepared the way for reading Emerson, which I regard as one of the chief privileges of my life. I owe more to Emerson than to any other writer or teacher. He occupies on the roll of fame a unique position as poet, philosopher, humourist, teacher, and brave citizen. His son, in a recent number of the *Bookman*, relates how, when he and his sisters were in bed, his "father would come up and, sitting by us in the twilight, chant, to our great delight, a good-night song, which he made up as he sang, to the trees, the birds, the flowers, the members of the family, and even the cow and the cat." Emerson lived a beautiful and a useful life, and, whether employed in interpreting Nature or the powers and possibilities of the human soul, and its necessary affinity to all suns or systems ; or lecturing to students ; or teaching the duties of lofty citizenship ; or, in his own words, "planting the rose of beauty on the brow of chaos " ; or chanting twilight melodies to his children, he is worthy of admiration as one of the luminaries of the human race.

From the time I lived in Manchester, when and where I heard Cobden and Bright address public meetings, I became an adherent of the Manchester School. In after years I had many opportunities to come into active contact with the leaders of the School, and the more I saw them and knew them the more I esteemed and admired them. It has been supposed by many that Cobden and Bright cared much more for the material prosperity than for the moral progress of the people. This is a mistake. I speak from experience, and say, without hesitation, that it mattered not whether the question discussed, or the object to be promoted by them, was domestic or international; it was always considered in the prevailing light of justice between man and man, and nation and nation. I admired these leaders for their great ability, still more for their unceasing and disinterested activity, and more than all for their loyalty to righteousness. I never knew an instance, or the fragment of an instance, where they surrendered principle to expediency, or subordinated conviction to party gain or personal popularity. They rendered immense service to the State by the economic revolution they mainly assisted to produce, and a service to mankind by advocating pacific methods to adjust international differences. Their service to the State was immediate, palpable, and lasting ; their service to mankind, though great, has, in a much greater degree, to be realised ; and it will be realised, as the ever-increasing necessities and aspirations for peace will gradually more and more influence the convictions, the conscience, and the conduct of nations.

IN LONDON.[1]

Soon after I came to London I commenced writing articles for

[1] A few weeks after I came to London I stopped one Sunday evening to

newspapers and periodicals, some of which were inserted and others were not; and some of those which were inserted were paid for, and others were not. But what I did after a time, and with more effect, though it brought no financial grist to the mill, was to join and take an active part in the formation and promotion of certain political and social organisations. At that time political reform societies were more real and more in earnest than, as a rule, they have been since. Parliamentary Reform Acts tranquillised a portion of the public mind, and diminished the necessity for political agitation; and subsequent experience has shown that there was more eagerness shown by many to get the suffrage than to use it with advantage when got. The nation is more indebted to committee work than is generally supposed. It frequently happens that some well-known man, in or out of Parliament, becomes the leader or chief mouthpiece of some public question, and gets the lion's, or more than the lion's, share of publicity or applause. But in many cases it is the less-known men who, unseen, in committee, arrange proceedings, discuss ways and means, prepare public meetings, provide suitable literature, and by various methods promote propagandist activity. It fell to my lot to mingle from time to time, mostly in committee action, with several reforming organisations. I was a member of the committee of the Early Closing Association; of the Society for the Abolition of Capital Punishment; of the Political and Financial Reform Association; of the Society for the Abolition of the Taxes on Knowledge; of the Society for the Suppression of the Opium Trade; of the Peace Society; of the Ballot Society; of the Committee for the Abolition of Flogging in the Army and Navy; and of more than one committee for the promotion of National Education. These societies did not exist and act simultaneously, but at different times from 1845 to 1880. Though officered generally by different persons at different times, the societies specified were in spirit and in aim parts of one whole.

listen to a speaker who was addressing an open-air meeting. With other things, he said he was prepared to prove that " eternity had a centre." Fixing his eyes particularly on me, and probably on my watch-chain, he said he felt sure that *one* gentleman present could follow the drift of his argument, the basis of which was that immediately anyone could form a definite idea of time, that moment would be the centre of eternity. At that moment a man by my side tipped over another man's hat immediately in front of us, when a scrimmage occurred, in which I was jolted about from right to left, and almost swept off my legs. I was glad enough to escape from the too demonstrative company, and soon found, to my bewilderment, that I was relieved of my watch. No doubt the speaker was in league with some of his listeners, and endeavoured to arrest my attention while others robbed me. I have had ample time since to meditate on " the centre of eternity," and take more care of my watch.

They sprang from similar necessities, were nurtured by similar motives, represented so many phases of the National Reform Movement, and assisted to educate the head and heart of the people.

A succinct account of the societies mentioned, with many of the well-known names connected with them, the work they did and the influence they exerted on legislation and national life, would make an interesting historical chapter. That is beyond my purpose or my power to supply. I may, however, mention one or two incidents. In 1848 Emerson visited this country, when he delivered several lectures in Manchester. I was at the time a member of the London Early Closing Association, which was in a state of monetary stagnation. Hearing that Emerson had arrived in London, I suggested that he should be invited to deliver two or three lectures for the benefit of the Association, and Mr. John Lilwall, its secretary, and I were appointed to wait on him. We did so, and were received with captivating courtesy. We told him how we were situated, and wanted to be lifted out of debt ; and we felt sure that he, by lecturing on our behalf, could do so. He hesitated, and said he was scarcely prepared to give any more lectures in England. I ventured to say that two or three of the lectures he had delivered in Manchester might be repeated to different audiences in London. In reply, he said he could not do so, and one reason was that if he were conscious, when lecturing in London, that one of his audience had heard him give the same lectures in Manchester, he should feel most uncomfortable—a proof of the peculiar sensitiveness of his nature. He, however, promised to think over the matter, and let us know his decision.

Two or three days after Emerson wrote and accepted our proposal, and undertook to give three lectures—the first on Montaigne, the second on Napoleon, and the third on Shake-speare. I need scarcely say the committee were delighted. Exeter Hall, at that time the most notable meeting-place in England, was taken, and the necessary preparations were made for the delivery of the lectures. The tickets of admission sold rapidly ; we had splendid audiences and gratifying results. After paying all expenses we netted £150, paid our debts, emerged from difficulty, blessed Emerson, and went on our way rejoicing. On the occasion of the last lecture I first saw Thomas Carlyle, at that time a dark, shaggy man, self-centred and impassive. He sat in the same position, with folded arms and crossed legs, and not moving a muscle during the delivery of the lecture. The audience now and then cheered the lecturer right heartily, while Carlyle sat still as a statue. The chair was occupied by Mr. Monckton Milnes, M.P. and poet, and afterwards, on the nomination of Lord Palmerston, Lord Houghton. Mr. Milnes, in returning thanks for thanks, said the audience at the moment was in the presence of three historic facts—namely, Emerson, Shakespeare, and Exeter Hall. He might have said four such facts by referring to the presence of Thomas Carlyle.

INTERNATIONALISM.

One of the memories I cherish is interwoven with some articles I wrote entitled " Two Sisters," the first of which appeared in the *People's Journal*, September 23rd, 1848. The two sisters were England and France, and the articles were written to show that there was no shadow of reason or necessity that the two nations should look at each other with smouldering suspicion or as "natural enemies," as many, on the platform and in the Press, strongly maintained at the time; but there was abundant reason and necessity why they should regard each other as natural friends. I said: "Why should two nations whose geographical positions were so contiguous, whose history moved on somewhat parallel lines, whose institutions were moulded by similar forces, who inherited and enjoyed a common civilisation, and who could, with equal advantage, and in a variety of ways, promote each other's welfare —why should two such nations look at each other with jealous or angry eyes and make vast preparations to check, counteract, or crush each other? Because, as nations, they have not consulted their best interests, or appreciated each other's nobler qualities." The articles were not altogether fruitless. Portions of them were, with the timely assistance of Joseph Sturge, translated into French and sent to French newspapers, and in several instances got friendly notice. This was followed by a collective visit of British workmen to Paris, which was succeeded by a return visit of two hundred Frenchmen to London. These were the first visits of the kind, and we are now happily getting familiar with them. It was very different when the articles on the "Two Sisters" were written fifty-seven years ago. Then, in vindicating the international sisterhood of England and France, it was as difficult to move against the stream of opinion as it is now getting easy to move with it. If so much progress has been effected in such a comparatively short space of time, are we not justified in expecting similar progress in future?

The general good feeling and understanding between England and the United States of America carry with them an alluring prospect. Though conflicting opinions and occasional frictions may arise between the two countries, another war between them is well-nigh impossible ; and this condition of things may be accepted as a permanent conquest of civilisation. What has been done by pacific inclinations and tendencies between England and the United States may be accomplished by England and France. Then England would be enabled to shake hands in perpetual friendship with the great Republic across the Atlantic and with another great Republic across the British Channel, and so present to the world another historic product of progress. And what England, France, and the United States may do during the present generation, other nations, to their immeasurable advantage, may imitate in riper times.[1]

Though the war spirit and war methods of destruction abound and press heavily on civilisation, they are hopefully assailed in many ways from many directions. Internationalism gradually gains ground. Numerous social and political activities, the conquering march of science around the world, reciprocal civic, economic, and journalistic hospitalities, mutual labour greetings and movements, and ever-increasing demands for political freedom in several nations, are all pacific in character and tendency. A scientific discovery in Germany or the United States soon becomes the inheritance of all nations. A notable book published in Russia or Norway or Holland is anticipated from sea to sea, and soon gets translated into half a dozen or half a score different languages. A remarkable work of art produced in one nation, whether it be picture, poem, musical or dramatic composition, elicits cosmopolitan smiles and cheers. The yearly Nobel £8,000 Peace Prize is, in seen and unseen ways, producing excellent results. Few things are more certain than the progress of democracy in many nations,

---

[1] A short time after I erected the Falmouth Hospital, and when I was presented with the honorary freedom of the borough in September, 1893, I said, at the complimentary dinner which followed, that, "as Cornwall was mainly surrounded by the sea, I should like, in the interests of sailors of all lands, to build a lighthouse somewhere on the Cornish coast ; and as there was a point near by—the Manacles, notorious for the disastrous shipwrecks they occasioned—it might be a fitting place for such a lighthouse ; and, if built, I should like to dedicate it to the memory of Couch Adams, the distinguished mathematician, and joint discoverer with Le Verrier of the planet Neptune. I should also like to pay a similar tribute of respect to Le Verrier, and erect to his memory a similar lighthouse on the coast of France. Such sister lighthouses, if erected, might complacently glance at each other, and mutually promote a friendly feeling between two sister nations—England and France." The matter was subsequently talked over with the Mayor and others of Falmouth, when it was decided that I should provide a free library for the town in preference to building a lighthouse.

and as a rule peace and democracy go hand in hand.   The socialists of Germany say they will not fight and kill the socialists of France; and it is within the limits of possibility that professing Christians, in the name of their Master, the Prince of Peace, may, as circumstances ripen, make a similar declaration.   Industrial development, a commanding fact and factor, is unmistakably pacific in effect; and the Labour Party—a great and growing party—is charged with a similar spirit.   In fact, civilised peoples are, year by year, getting more civilised, and kings, presidents, cabinet ministers, and ambassadors are, from necessity as well as inclination, getting more and more conciliatory in their active policy.   Much, if not most, of what is best *in* human nature is making for what is best *for* human nature, and the altruistic dreams of one age ripen into realisations in succeeding times.

THE CHARTIST AGITATION AND PHYSICAL FORCE.

The Chartist agitation, accompanied by certain threats of violence, caused public anxiety in 1848, when extensive preparations were made by the Chartist party to hold simultaneously three "great demonstrations" on April 10th of that year.   One of these was held in Manchester to represent the North of England, one in Nottingham to represent the Midland Counties, and the other in London, under the leadership of Fergus O'Connor, to represent the Southern Counties.   The Duke of Wellington, commander-in-chief at the time, made ample and paraded preparations to meet possible contingencies.   It so happened that I had to go to Nottingham on business on Saturday, April 8th.   When I got there I found the town in a considerable state of commotion on account of a great preliminary Chartist meeting about to be held in the market-place.   Having done my business as I best could in the disturbed state of the town, I went to the meeting, and, after listening to two or three somewhat fiery speeches, I pushed my way to the wagon platform and asked leave, as a stranger from London, to speak.   My request was readily granted.   With youthful courage I mounted the platform, expressed sympathy with the principles of the people's charter, but strongly deprecated physical force in any form as a means to obtain it.   Instead of evoking opposition, as I expected, I found a majority agreed with me.   When leaving the crowd and about to return to London, a gentleman (Bean by name) asked me whether I could make it convenient to remain and address much greater meetings at Loughborough on the following day (Sunday) and in Nottingham the day following. I said I was not prepared to do so, my means not allowing it.   He pressed his application, and, two or three others having encouraged him, he said he would gladly pay my hotel expenses if I remained. Being told that my speech had a pacifying effect, and fascinated with my new experience and the spirit of battle, I consented to stay. I went to Loughborough on the Sunday as agreed, was again permitted to address the great open-air meeting, and received a warmer welcome than I did the day before. But the greatest meeting of all in the Midland Counties, and the one which caused most local anxiety, was held on Monday, the memorable April 10th, in Nottingham, and which I was *invited* to address. I did so, and condemned more emphatically than before the use of violence in any form to gain political ends. While the meeting was being held the soldiers, who were picketed in the town to preserve order, marched through the market-place and produced a temporary scare. But they were not wanted, as nine-tenths of the multitude assembled were much more inclined to deal in words than blows. So ended my first political contest.

INTERNATIONAL PEACE CONGRESS.

Of the many public questions discussed fifty or sixty years ago (and since) the peace question, with its immeasurable possibilities, interested me the most. I naturally desired to attend the Brussels Peace Congress in September, 1848, but did not expect to do so, as I was not able to meet the necessary expenses. But a few days before the Congress met I received, to my surprise and delight, a letter from Henry Richard (afterwards M.P.), the secretary of the London Peace Society, saying that his committee, in consideration of the assistance I rendered the peace movement, and particularly the speeches I delivered at Chartist meetings in Nottinghamshire, offered me a free delegate's ticket to Brussels and back and free lodgings there during the Congress. The joyful news saluted me like the sunshine of a June morning. I accepted the offer with suitable thanks, and went with about 150 other delegates from this country to the *first* International Peace Congress, with Cobden, "The International Man," as its chief ornament and spokesman. One of the delegates to the Congress was Mr. John Bradley, ex-mayor of Nottingham, who informed me that, after I left the town about six months before, it was resolved to thank me for my courageous conduct and speeches, that £10 was collected to be presented to me, and that the thanks and the money had not been sent because my address was not known. Mr. Bradley then and there, to my surprise and delight, presented me with £10. I felt as if fortune had showered on me special favours—first in having my expenses as a delegate to the Congress paid, and secondly to receive, without expectation, such a—to me at the time—splendid present !

The Brussels Congress was a success. It received the active support of the Belgian Prime Minister, the patronising smile of the Belgian King, a considerable share of public attention, and the good wishes of the lovers of mankind everywhere. That Peace Congress, though it encountered opposition, and got pelted with sneers, was historic, as it was the first of the kind, and it sowed seed which has since germinated, and from which may now be seen the prospect of an international harvest. Just fifty years after— and fifty years are not much in the life of nations—Government representatives from the independent nations of Europe and America met at The Hague, in response to an invitation from the Czar of Russia, to consider and afterwards to sanction the general truthfulness and applicability of the principles enunciated at the Brussels Congress, and to suggest methods for their practical adoption. Had the South African Republics been represented at the Hague Conference, as they wished to be, or had Kruger's repeated appeals to submit the matters in dispute to arbitration been adopted, South Africa would not have been blasted by British power ; we should not have entered on a costly and cowardly war, and thereby weakened our position in the world, incurred the reproach, and called down the general condemnation of civilised peoples.

Two other International Peace Congresses, under the guidance of the same committee, with Cobden as leader, took place—one at Paris in 1849, and the other at Frankfort-on-the-Main in 1850. I attended both, and on each occasion paid my own expenses, as in the meantime I had made some financial headway. The Paris Congress, with Victor Hugo as chairman, was a complete success. Having a few months before written a biographical sketch of Lamartine, which appeared in the *People's Journal*, and knowing that he had married an English lady, I summoned up sufficient courage to call on him, and was granted a short and sweet inter- view. I presented him with a copy of the *People's Journal* con- taining the biographical sketch, which he accepted with stately politeness. He said he was an admirer of English institutions, and that he cordially hoped the Peace Congress then sitting would produce good fruit. It so happened that on the same day the members of the Congress, in answer to a special invitation from M. de Tocqueville, attended a reception at the Foreign Office. It also happened that M. de Tocqueville had married an English lady, and I said, when I had the privilege of being introduced to him, as two French Ministers who immediately succeeded each other in the Foreign Office had married English ladies, I hoped it would assist to unite England and France in the bonds of peace. He replied in excellent English, and warmly expressed a similar desire. That desire has recently received partial fulfilment in improved relationships between the two countries.

ALSO WORTH REMEMBERING.

Another reference to Cobden may be interesting. In 1859 Cobden went to the United States to investigate and protect a substantial interest he had in an American railway. During his absence Lord Palmerston was appointed to form a new Ministry, and without the opportunity of consulting Cobden nominated him President of the Board of Trade. This was before the days of submarine telegraphy. In due time Cobden returned to England, when a deputation from the Political and Financial Reform Association was appointed to wait on him and present him with a congratulatory address. The deputation consisted of James Stansfeld, afterwards M.P. for Halifax, and more than once Cabinet Minister; of Sir Arthur Hayter, afterwards M.P. and Chairman of Ways and Means; of Samuel Morley, afterwards M.P. for Bristol, and who subsequently declined a peerage; of James White, afterwards M.P. for Brighton, and of myself, afterwards M.P. for Salisbury. Cobden was staying for the day with Charles Gilpin, M.P., at 10, Bedford Square, where the deputation had appointed to meet him. When we called he had just returned from an interview with Palmerston. He gave us a most interesting account of the interview, and among other things said that when formally offered office he respectfully declined it; and one reason he gave was that he might not agree with all his lordship's policy, and if he did not he should resign office, and thereby probably cause inconvenience. Cobden also said he ventured to mention the name of the Hon. C. Pelham Villiers, an able man with considerable Parliamentary experience, and that he also spoke of the substantial qualities of Charles Gilpin. The result was that both Villiers and Gilpin were appointed members of the new Government; and so Cobden, though he declined office himself, promoted others to office. I may add that some years before, when offered a baronetcy at the suggestion of Lord John Russell, Cobden declined the honour.

I ought not, even in these scrappy notes, to omit the names of Elihu Burritt and George Thompson, with whom, in the Press, in committee work, and at public meetings, I frequently acted. Elihu Burritt was known as "the learned blacksmith," who left the anvil in America and came to this country in answer to an invitation from Mr. Joseph Sturge. I worked heartily with Burritt in producing and circulating his *Bond of Brotherhood*, and took part with him in many meetings preparatory to holding International Peace Congresses. He, in fact, was the originator of these Congresses, and is, or will be, entitled in the years to come to occupy a niche in the Temple of Peace, when it is built up and established; and it will most assuredly be built up and established, because it is in harmony with the deepest and divinest human interests. I also co-operated with Elihu Burritt in holding and addressing public meetings to establish an International Penny Postage—a movement which has since made substantial progress under the able direction of Henniker Heaton, M.P., and which must, in cousinship with other cosmopolitan ideas, make corresponding progress in future.

I was also brought into frequent contact, journalistically and in committees, with George Thompson, who earned fame during the early part of the last century as an orator on anti-slavery platforms. When Lloyd Garrison, the distinguished American anti-slavery advocate, came to this country in 1867, I suggested that he should be invited to what may now be called a historical breakfast party in St. James's Hall. The meeting was held and addressed by John Bright, who occupied the chair, by Lord John Russell, the Duke of Argyle, J. Stuart Mill, Lord Granville, William V. Harcourt, Lloyd Garrison, and George Thompson. Mr. Bright, in one of the greatest speeches even he ever delivered, when referring to the anti-slavery struggle and the anti-slavery war just concluded in America, spoke of Wendell Phillips as "the greatest orator that speaks the English tongue." Mr. Bright was probably not aware that Lord Brougham, in a speech delivered in Exeter Hall nearly forty years before, applied almost the same words to George Thompson. It was a singular coincidence that the greatest English orator of the day should have described the greatest American orator in almost the same language as was, with authority, applied to the greatest English orator of a preceding generation, and who was then on the platform in the eightieth year of his age. Had George Thompson been a rich or well-to-do man instead of being a poor man, he might, and no doubt would, have occupied a distinguished place in our Parliamentary history. As it was, he was returned as member of Parliament many years before for the Tower Hamlets, with the greatest majority then on record. His speech at this meeting was the last he ever delivered, and the speech of Mr. William Harcourt, afterwards Chancellor of the Exchequer and Leader of the Liberal party in the House of Commons, was the first he delivered in London.

As reminiscent of the central years of the last century, I may say I heard Sir Robert Peel deliver his great speech on the third reading of his Bill for the repeal of the Corn Laws in 1846, and the following year I heard Daniel O'Connell deliver his last speech in the House of Commons, when his voice was so weak that he could only be heard with difficulty in the gallery. During those central years I corresponded with Father Mathew, Robert Owen, Leigh Hunt, Harriet Martineau, Joseph Mazzini, Mrs. Beecher Stowe, and Sir William Molesworth. I saw Macready in the character of Hamlet when he left the stage in 1851. I heard Thackeray deliver his lectures on "The English Humourists of the Eighteenth Century," and afterwards his lectures on "The Four Georges," in the Surrey Gardens Hall; and I also heard Dickens give his first series of public readings. I was present when Cobden and the Duke of Wellington shook hands, amid rapturous applause, at the opening of the first International Exhibition in Hyde Park in 1851. Walter Savage Landor has somewhere said that he exulted in the thought that he had shaken hands with Kosciusco, and that fifty years after he felt equal satisfaction in shaking hands with Kossuth. I felt equal satisfaction in being present at a meeting in the Hanover Square Rooms and shaking hands with Kossuth and Mazzini, and felt still more honoured by a passing call from Garibaldi when he visited London somewhat meteorically in 1864. I was a member of his Reception Committee.

A Struggle, a Failure, and a Triumph.

I now come to a turning-point in life. I thought that, if I could write for periodicals owned by others, I might start and own one myself; and to that end I directed and shaped my actions. It was no easy matter, more than half a century ago, when the taxes on knowledge were in full swing, and before modern Education Acts came into operation, to commence and establish a magazine, with experience and without capital, or with capital and without experience; and, of course, doubly more difficult to achieve success without both money and experience. This I attempted to do without success. I tested my ability by commencing in January, 1850, *The Public Good*. The magazine was published for a short time by Charles Gilpin. But to avoid publishing commission, and to economise in other ways, I became my own publisher. For that purpose I rented a room of Isaac Pitman Brothers, phonographers, Paternoster Row, for which I paid four shillings a week. In this room I acted as editor, publisher, and advertisement canvasser. Here I worked during the day, and slept on a mattress spread on the little counter at night-time. My sleep, however, was frequently broken by cabs, trade vans, and other vehicles rattling over the granite pavement of the narrow Row. This so enfeebled my health that I had to remove to other rooms near by, where I increased my publishing responsibilities and anxieties by starting and editing other periodicals, in the hope that they would mutually advertise and assist each other. If nature had not provided me with a good constitution, I could not have survived the stress and storm of those days. What I did and how I struggled against the stream for three or four years until I got temporarily submerged, and how I again got on my feet and conquered, and more than conquered, lost ground, may be seen by the following report, reproduced from the *City Press* of November 4th, 1866 :—

BANQUET TO J. PASSMORE EDWARDS, Esq.

A gathering of more than usual interest took place on Monday, October 29th, 1866, at the Albion Tavern, Aldersgate Street, when Mr. Passmore Edwards was invited by a number of his friends to a banquet given in his honour. Mr. John Hodge, of the firm of Spalding & Hodge, occupied the chair.

After the complimentary toasts were given, the Chairman rose to propose the toast of the evening. He said : Gentlemen, an Albion Tavern dinner is an ordinary, every-day affair ; it is also a pleasant and enjoyable one when the company is as I see around this table. Our present meeting, agreeable as it is, takes place under circumstances *extraordinary* and unique. We are honoured by the presence of Mr. Passmore Edwards as our guest on this occasion, a gentleman who, as you know, has for many years been connected with literature and the Press. About fifteen years ago Mr. Passmore Edwards —acting, I believe, somewhat under the advice of his friend Mr. Charles Gilpin, now M.P. for Northampton—started several publications, periodical and otherwise, of great interest and merit, and which had a considerable circulation. Many gentlemen present know full well the fascination and difficulties incidental to publishing, and how uncertain is the result in very many cases. After a few years Mr. Passmore Edwards found himself out of his depth ; and a severe illness coming on, at a time when health and energy were indispensable to his extrication, he was at length compelled to relinquish the struggle. Acting under the advice of friends, he gave up all that he had to those to whom he was indebted, receiving from them a release from their claims, together with their sympathy for what I believe was generally considered the result of *unavoidable misfortune.* After this Mr. Passmore Edwards continued to work on for more than ten years, and at length, by the blessing of Almighty God on his talents, industry, energy, and perseverance, he found himself in a position to do that which had all along been the object of his intense desire and ambition—namely, to pay to his late creditors those sums from which, although *legally* released, he considered himself under a moral obligation to pay, if ever it should be in his power ; and, accordingly, not long since, Mr. Passmore Edwards *revived* and paid his bygone debts. Gentlemen, we are here this evening to thank him for his generous and liberal conduct, to tell him how highly we appreciate the motives by which he has been actuated, and to do homage to so noble an instance of uprightness and conscientiousness. We are here, also, to present to Mr. Passmore Edwards a testimonial, of comparatively small pecuniary value, it is true, but still a testimonial and token of our admiration and approbation of his highly honourable conduct. Mr. Passmore Edwards, in the name of the subscribers and of the present company, I have the honour and pleasure to present to you this watch and chain—the inscription being, " Presented to J. Passmore Edwards, Esq., October 29th, 1866, by friends who have special and unusual occasion to testify their appreciation of his integrity and uprightness." Gentlemen, I beg to propose " The Health of Mr. J. Passmore Edwards," wishing him long life, happiness, and continued prosperity.

Mr. Edwards, who, on rising, was received with loud and long-continued applause, said : This ovation, if I may so call it, brings out in strong contrast the period when I came to London about twenty years ago. I was then a very young man with only a few shillings in my pocket, and I could not boast of having a single friend. But, though I was poor in pocket, I was rich in hope. I may say that my head and heart were as buoyant with enthusiastic dreams as my purse was light ; but, though woefully lacking the needful, I determined to establish a periodical, thinking that I should be enabled thereby to build up a fortune, if not win fame. Alas ! how the dreams of youth melt away before the touch of rugged experience ! By dint of frugality, I managed to scrape together fifty pounds ; and, after elaborate preparations, I wrote my prospectus and launched my first literary enterprise, which was a monthly magazine called *The Public Good*. But how could I commence operations with such slender means ? I did as too many have done before me—I worked on credit. Mr. Charles Gilpin, having confidence in me, gave me a note of introduction to you, sir, and you gave me credit for paper. Though *The Public Good* [1] sold several thousands monthly, and though I received congratulations and thanks from different parts of the country, the magazine did not pay. Finding the magazine did not pay, I brought out another, hoping that the second would prop up the first ; but by so doing I only diluted my ability and increased my

---

[1] That *The Public Good* was serviceable in its day and generation may be seen in the following extracts from letters which came to hand unexpectedly within a few days of each other. Mr. Sherwood Smith, the Chairman of the Bristol Branch of the National Peace Congress, in a letter dated April 22nd, 1905, inviting me to the annual Congress about to be held in Bristol, says :— " It was to you, through *The Public Good*, nearly sixty years ago, that I became specially interested in this kind of Christian work, and of other causes now marching in the right direction." A few days after I received a letter, dated May 7th, 1905, from Mr. William Tebb, Rede Hall, Surrey, who says :—" As your monthly magazine, *The Public Good*, was the first to direct my attention to humanitarian reforms about sixty years ago, I am sending, for your kind acceptance, a copy of the second edition of my book [*Premature Burial*] on an important but much-neglected subject. A Bill has been prepared to lay before Parliament with the object of putting an end to the tragic occurrences described in the volume, and to which we are all more or less liable." I have received from time to time during the last fifty-five years hundreds of similar letters.

difficulties. While I met my bills my credit was good to almost any extent, and I went on for three or four years, bringing out periodical after periodical. One of my magazines was called *The Poetic Companion.* You may imagine my inexperience and hopefulness by devoting a magazine entirely to poetry. Another of my works was called *The Biographical Magazine,* devoted exclusively to biography, a far more practical enterprise; another was devoted to peace, called *The Peace Advocate;* and another was devoted entirely to the young. But the more works I published the deeper I got into debt, until I found myself tossing about in a nice little sea of difficulties to the tune of several thousands of pounds. I was my own editor, my own publisher, my own clerk, and my own advertisement agent. In fact, I undertook too much. At last my health and strength failed me. I struggled against the tide as long as I could, until wave after wave went over my head and submerged me. Whether I should have recovered my feet had not ill-health disabled me I cannot say. But I was obliged to absent myself from the office for some time; and, being the mainspring of action, I was no sooner removed than everything was brought to a standstill. You, sir, kindly came to my bedside, and advised me what to do. As no time was to be lost—periodical works must be out to the day—it was decided to sell the copyrights and stock, which was done, as I thought then, and as I think now, at a great sacrifice. When I was strong enough to return to the office, after an absence of about ten weeks, I found that my poor estate was almost wound up, and that it yielded 5s. in the pound. This composition was accepted by my creditors, and they all, with one exception, gave me a receipt in full of all demands. They took a generous view of my position, and thought that I had suffered a reverse of fortune from no moral fault of my own, and that I was rather entitled to sympathy than condemnation.

Now I come to what I may consider the darkest period of my life. I had lost my credit, my health was impaired; I had fought and failed; but from the hour of my defeat, or I may now say of my repulse, I cherished an unfaltering resolve to redeem my credit and pay everyone in full. I put this one intention in the very front of my life, and disciplined all my actions in obedience to its fulfilment. Just like the fugitive slave who keeps the north star steadily in view when escaping from bondage, I felt that while my promises were unredeemed I was in slavery. I longed to be free. This was the pole-star of my life, from which I never diverted my gaze, and towards which I directed all my hopes and shaped all my actions. I need not enter into a history of my hopes, of my struggles and my fears. Suffice it to say that in the course of time, by working on and wasting not, I recovered lost ground and appropriated the very first-fruits of my improved position to pay my just debts. I felt that I had left a work I had undertaken to do in an unfinished state; that I had incurred liabilities which I had not met; that I had succumbed to circumstances when circumstances should have succumbed to me. I therefore determined to wrestle with these circumstances, and put them, if possible, under my feet. Another motive related to my creditors. I felt that every man should be as good as his word. I promised to pay, and I felt bound to fulfil that promise, if it were at the expense of inconvenience or sacrifice; and I maintain that no lapse of time, no statute of limitations, no receipts in full, no legal release, not even insolvent debtors' courts or Queen's Bench prisons, can pay just debts. We live in an essentially commercial age. Commerce is the source, the primal source, of our national prosperity, and the virtues of our people depend to a great extent on the manner in which that commerce is conducted. Englishmen, in fact, breathe an atmosphere of commerce, and this atmosphere presses upon us on every side, and penetrates into the details of our daily life. Every man, then, should be interested in keeping that atmosphere pure, for by so doing he is assisting to give a healthy tone to society, and to maintain our national credit. When Mr. W. H. Collingridge spoke to me about a testimonial, he said it would be something that I might transmit to posterity. I almost smiled at the suggestion, for the thought of posterity never crossed my imagination. Sufficient for me is the duty of to-day. It is only the rare and gifted few who can perform deeds the memory of which shall live beyond the present; but it is in the power of every man, be he ever so humble, to influence by his example, for good or for evil, the circle in which he lives and moves. This is what I have endeavoured to do; and I feel more than rewarded by the satisfaction of my own conscience and the enthusiastic feelings evoked around this banquet board to-night. I thank you, gentlemen, from the bottom of my heart for this testimonial and generous greeting. I shall preserve the testimonial as a memento of your kindness, and I shall treasure the memory of this greeting with my brightest and most enduring recollections.

Other speakers followed, including W. H. Collingridge, of the *City Press;* Jos. Newton, of the Royal Mint; John Francis, of the *Athenæum;* E. J. Reed, Chief Constructor of the Navy; R. W. Edis, President of the Architectural Association; Mr. William Spicer; and among those who wrote expressing their sympathy with the object of the meeting were Charles Gilpin, M.P., Samuel Morley, Thomas Hood, and William Howitt.

How, it has been asked, did you get so securely on your feet again? By working hard and waiting, by contributing to newspapers and magazines, and so accumulating experience; and, after a time, becoming manager and then proprietor of the *Mechanics' Magazine*, a weekly threepenny periodical which had existed for about half a century, but, at the time I took it in hand, was in low water. I subsequently became the proprietor of the *Building News*, which was commenced a few years before by Messrs. Kelly, of the *London Directory*. As neither of these periodicals was paying when I took command, I was enabled to become their proprietor on easy terms, and by careful husbandry of time and resources I was fortunate enough to make both successful. Then I felt for the first time in a fair field, with my hands at the plough and my head in the sunlight and the breeze. I afterwards became proprietor of several other periodicals. How different things might have been had I such a chance fourteen or fifteen years before. Then, in all probability, the central and most vigorous portion of my life would have been much more productive, and I should not have had to struggle so unsuccessfully and to fall by the way—but luckily to rise again. The more strenuous the fight against adverse circumstances, the greater the conquest when they are subdued and removed.

D

Propagandist Pamphlets.

I may here refer to three pamphlets I published during the fifties of the last century. One was entitled *Intellectual Tollbars*, another *The Triple Curse*, and the other *The War : A Blunder and a Crime*. *Intellectual Tollbars* was written to promote the repeal of what were called "the taxes on knowledge." No paper of any kind could be made in those days, either for printing or any other purpose, without paying a heavy tax ; no advertisement, great or small, could appear in any newspaper or periodical without paying one shilling and sixpence duty ; and no copy of any newspaper, of any size or price, could be produced and circulated without the Government impressed stamp of one penny. These taxes enfeebled the paper-making, bookmaking, printing, and publishing trades, and acted as a general deterrent to the advancement of education and the spread of knowledge. The repeal of these taxes, after a long and strenuous agitation, liberated and vastly increased the prosperity of the industries employed, and imparted a new impulse to the national mind. In fact, the removal of the taxes mentioned was as advantageous to the producers of paper, books, newspapers, and magazines of all kinds, printing inks and printing machinery, as the repeal of the Corn Laws benefited the general condition of the country. I need scarcely say that the great Anti-Corn Law and Free Trade leaders, who a few years before shed undiminishing lustre on their age and nation, were also the leaders of the movement for the repeal of the taxes on knowledge. As Cobden and Bright had the largest share of public appreciation and applause for the leading part they took in repealing the bread tax, it was arranged by them and others that Milner Gibson, their able coadjutor, should pilot the Bills involving the taxes on knowledge through the Commons. And this was done with marked success. No one, unless liberally endowed with the prophetic spirit, could have predicted that the repeal of the taxes on knowledge would prepare the way for such prodigious results ; or that where one copy of a book or newspaper or publication was produced then, more than thirty times the number would be produced forty or fifty years after. Neither could he have discerned that so many newspapers would, in the meantime, be owned or adroitly used by monetary magnates for capitalistic or social aggrandisement. Herein may be seen a lurking danger, which will have to be closely watched and counteracted, or the commonwealth will suffer.

The pamphlet entitled *The Triple Curse* pointed out the evil effects of the opium trade on India, where opium was produced by British cultivators ; on China, into which it was smuggled by British merchants; and on England, the author and promoter of the great wrong. Mr. Montgomery Martin, who was for many years the British Treasurer in China, said before a Select Committee of the House of Commons : "The opium trade is desolating China, corrupting its government, and bringing the fabric of that extra-ordinary empire to a state of desolation." I proved this by a host of facts and authorities in my pamphlet, which passed through more than one edition. The other pamphlet, *The War : A Blunder and a Crime*, dealt with the British and French war against Russia in the Crimea. Every position I then assumed has since been strengthened by established facts. We commenced that war, with France as an ally, to break and roll back the power of Russia, and, in Lord Palmerston's language, " to maintain the integrity and independence of the Turkish Empire." A huge, far-reaching mis-calculation. Russia was not rolled back, and has since been advancing east and west. The integrity and independence of Turkey were less secure after than before the war. France, our ally then, is the ally of Russia now. By that war we antagonised Russia for generations, and have since had to pay the penalty, in one shape or another, to the tune of millions sterling annually. We expended directly on the war more than a hundred millions sterling, and sacrificed forty thousand human lives, or—as John Bright said at the time—as many grown-up men as were living in Birmingham. Mr. Kinglake estimated that, from first to last, more than half a million of men perished through that war ; and Lord Salisbury, some years after, when commenting on the war, said, in sporting phraseology, that we made a mistake, and " put our money on the wrong horse."

THE ROMANCE OF TRIFLES.

During the fifties I occasionally lectured for mechanics' institutions and political societies, on three subjects particularly, which were respectively entitled "The Romance of Trifles," "Ways and Means," and "They who Rock the Cradle Rule the World." In the first-mentioned subject, which I refer to as a sample, I showed that big things were composed of little things ; that the mole-hill, the mountain, the globe, the solar system, and the starry universe consisted of a finite number of atoms ; that the character and quality of the greatest things depended on the character and quality of their smallest component parts ; that years, ages, and æons were divisible into minutes; that as it was with material things and time, so with human life ; that universal humanity—past, present, and to come—has been, and will be, made up of so many individuals, and the life of each individual is mainly built up of little things. The passing minute often governs succeeding minutes and hours. How desirable, then, that minutes, for their own sake and for that of their successors, should be well utilised! "Take care of the pennies, and the pounds will take care of themselves." It may be said with equal propriety: "Take care of the minutes, and the hours and days will take care of themselves." Selden says: "Syllables govern the world." Trifles light as air not only carry on their wings the seeds of big consequences to individuals, but sometimes assist in giving a new direction to national life. It is recorded that during the early and unpopular days of Mahomet he had to fly from his pursuers, who threatened to take his life. In his flight he entered and found shelter in a narrow-mouthed cave, over which a spider, during the following night, spun its web. His pursuers the next morning, seeing the web, did not enter and search the cave. Had they done so, and found Mahomet, the history and destiny of many Eastern nations might have been different to what they have been. It is also recorded that Oliver Cromwell, not liking the storm-brewing condition of things in England preparatory to the Commonwealth, made preparations to join his emigrant friends in America. But a dream diverted his thoughts, altered his purpose, and induced him to stay in England. But for that dream, British history might have assumed a different aspect. It is also recorded that Christopher Columbus, after many unsuccessful efforts to get help to go and discover another continent which he felt sure existed on the other side of the world, was about to abandon the project in despair. One day, in one of his wanderings, he lost his way, and, not knowing in what direction he should go, at last decided to follow the direction of a flying flock of birds. After a long walk he came to a monastery, where he found refuge and a friend in the father abbot, who gave him an introduction to Queen Isabella of Spain. The Queen encouraged Columbus, championed his enterprise, and, it is said, went so far as to pawn her jewels to expedite his immortal voyage of discovery. Had the birds referred to been shot, or otherwise slaughtered, to gratify some sporting passion, the fate and fame of Columbus might have been different, and the condition and prospects of the Old World and the New World might not have undergone such rapid development.

A BARBARIC CHALLENGE.

I may here refer to an incident which may assist to point a moral, if inadequate to adorn a tale. In 1862, in one of the journals under my control, I condemned Du Chaillu, the African traveller, for an insult he committed on a member of a London scientific society, and blamed Captain Burton (afterwards Sir Richard Burton) for his partial vindication of the offence. A few days after I received a formal visit from Captain Blakeley, who handed me a challenge from Captain Burton to meet him in a duel! Captain Blakeley was well known at the time as the inventor of a method for strengthening field-guns. I had to accept the challenge, offer an apology, or do nothing. I decided to do nothing. No doubt Captain Burton, with his old-world notions, thought he sufficiently vindicated his honour by so challenging me in due form, as I heard no more about it. I, on the other hand, thought that I as effectively defended myself by treating his hostile message with contemptuous silence. But suppose the matter developed differently? Suppose we were equally foolish and about equal in man-killing ability, that we fought and one or both of us got killed or wounded? Would right or reason or truth or honour have been thereby vindicated? Not a jot. But we were not equal in killing ability. Burton was a soldier, and doubtless a good marksman. I was neither, and had we pistol-shotted each other it would not have been right or reason or justice or law that would have triumphed, but superior marksmanship! War and duelling owe their existence to the same barbaric origin. Duelling is war between two persons ; war is duelling between two nations. Duelling, thanks to the good sense of the nation, is now made a criminal and punishable offence ; and war, in due time, by the good sense of the *nations*, will undergo similar disapproval and extinction.

THE "ECHO."

In 1868 Messrs. Cassell, Petter, & Galpin started the *Echo*, the first halfpenny daily newspaper published in London, with Arthur Arnold, afterwards chairman of the London County Council, as editor. After maintaining the paper for about seven years, and not succeeding with it as they expected, Messrs. Cassell & Co. sold it to Albert Grant, who, at the time, was supposed to be a millionaire. Mr. Grant within twelve months got tired of the responsibility and loss entailed, and sold the property, somewhat damaged in condition and value, to me. I soon, however, repented of the bargain, as I found the machinery and everything connected with the production of the paper, including even the foundations of the building itself, had to be renewed at the cost of several thousand pounds. For two or three years I staggered under my new obligations. But with diligence, fledged with hope, the paper gradually grew prosperous, and became a substantial London daily organ. In 1884 I sold two-thirds of the property to Mr. Andrew Carnegie and Mr. Samuel Story, M.P. But, differences having arisen over matters of opinion and methods of management, I bought back the said two-thirds, once more assumed full command, and remained proprietor and editor for twelve more years. I then sold the paper to a syndicate formed for the purpose. Afterwards the proprietorship and management of the *Echo* underwent other changes, until it ceased to exist in August, 1905.

During my fifty years' connection with newspapers and magazines I took a part—a subordinate one, I admit—in all the principal controversies on social and political questions of the time. I need scarcely say that I not infrequently found myself with struggling minorities, many of which, after adequate discussion, expanded into triumphant majorities. If a public question is reasonable and in harmony with general interests, it only requires, on the part of its defenders, time, courage, and suitable treatment, to secure social or legal sanction. Few things to me have been more pleasing or more historically picturesque than the having witnessed many national questions, fanned by agitation, emerge from obscurity, grow into "great facts," and blossom into Acts of Parliament. In all my experience as editor of, or contributor to, newspapers or magazines, I never wrote a sentence or passed a sentence on to the printers that I did not think true, and useful because true. While some editors and writers are ever ready to trim their sails to kiss, or to be kissed by, the passing breeze, in whatever way it may be moving, I always said, or caused to be said, where I had control, what I considered truest, whether popular at the time or not. What is best for mankind, now or in the future, is best for the nation, and what is best for the nation is best for individuals. I do not say I have not made mistakes, or, if at times I had been better informed, that I should not have written, spoken, or acted differently; but I do say—and I take no credit for saying or doing it—that I have always treated public questions purely in the light of general and enduring interests. And I would again act on the same principle and exalt it into an unshakable policy, though it might leave me, as it frequently did, in the company of the minority. Unfortunately, thousands of articles published annually in metropolitan newspapers are written to order, and do not carry with them the convictions of their writers, as thousands of votes are given annually in Parliament, not for the public, but for party good. There are "bulls" and "bears" as numerous and as unscrupulous, if not as cunning, on the newspaper Press as on 'Change. Day by day many dance to tunes played on newspaper organs for private gain at the public expense. But the claims of humanity, being transcendently greater than the claims of individuals or combinations of individuals, should exercise corresponding sway over individual conduct, and particularly in the realm of journalism.

ANOTHER CARLYLE REMINISCENCE.

Soon after the news of the Turkish atrocities in Bulgaria startled the world, a big London committee was formed to organise public opinion to denounce Turkish rule in Europe, and to condemn Disraeli in consequence of his Turkish proclivities. Scores of public meetings were held, and the greatest of them in St. James's Hall, which was presided over by the Duke of Westminster and addressed by Mr. Gladstone. Knowing that Thomas Carlyle shared our views, it was decided to ask him to take the chair at this meeting, and I was appointed to see him on the subject. I did so, and found him obliging, but in broken health. He expressed his inability to preside, much as he agreed with our action. He said : "My work is done, and I shall not be sorry when the Almighty takes me to Himself"—words, coming from such a source, well worth remembering. The name of John Bright being mentioned, Carlyle warmed up, and said he did not like John Bright, as many years before he was in his company and considered him an egotistic man. I said I had known Bright for many years, and co-operated with him in many ways, and always found him otherwise. "Ah," said Carlyle with pathos, "perhaps I was mistaken, and may have misjudged him ; and, if so, I should be sorry." When Disraeli's name was mentioned, the old sage's attitude stiffened, and, weak and weary as he was, and putting warmth and energy into his words, he spoke with scorn of Disraeli and his leadership of the Conservative party. Among other things he said : "I wonder how long this pretentious Jew will be allowed to dance on John Bull's body." And this, it should be remembered, was said some time after Disraeli had offered Carlyle a titular distinction—an offer that was politely declined. He preferred to remain what he had made himself, without Court recognition or adornment of any kind.

A Candidate for Parliament.

Well remembering the rejoicing in Cornwall over the passing of the Reform Bill in 1832, and taking part, as I did, in promoting the Reform Bill of 1867, it might be expected that, like hundreds of others, I should be smitten with a desire to get into the new reformed Parliament. I received, and accepted, an invitation to contest Truro in 1868, when the chances were decidedly against me. The character and colour of my political creed at the time may be seen from the following extract from my address:—"I would repeal the rate-paying clauses of the last Reform Bill; I would place the means of education within the reach of every child in the Kingdom; I am in favour of the ballot and an equalised distribution of Parliamentary constituencies; I would insist on a wise economy in every department of the State; I would endeavour to apply the teachings of Cobden, and cultivate a policy of non-intervention, and, wherever possible, substitute arbitration for war in the settlement of national disputes; I would abolish the purchase system in the army; I would put an end to the game laws; I would make the privileges of our national universities accessible to men of every religious creed; I would do my best to make the colonies self-supporting; I would abolish death punishments; and I would vote for an equalisation of the poor law and a more useful administration of charitable endowments. There are other social questions which would claim my attention, such as improved dwellings for the working classes, the institution of courts of arbitration for the protection of the funds of all legally constituted trade societies, and the cultivation of waste lands and revision of the licensing system." My address, written thirty-seven years ago, carried too much reform sail to captivate a majority of Truro electors. Besides, Truro, in 1868, returned two members, and every voter had two votes, and I had to sustain a contest single-handed against the old members, both connected with powerful county families—one a Conservative, and the other a Liberal—who offered themselves for re-election, and who united their forces to secure my defeat. The main points of my address carry with them now a flavour of ancient history, as most of them have since been embodied in legislation. Sir F. M. Williams, my chief opponent, left me between three and four hundred votes below him at the poll. His political creed was locally successful then; mine, in the main, has been nationally triumphant since.

IN PARLIAMENT.

I made no other attempt to enter Parliament until 1880, when I was invited to contest Salisbury, and where, after a vigorous fight, I conquered, in company with Mr. W. H. Grenfell, of Taplow Court ; and so another cherished aspiration got realised. I found stimulation in the thought that the poor Cornish boy, after many buffetings with fortune, should represent a cathedral city in Parliament. The satisfaction, however, which accompanied success was tempered by the knowledge that I was selected as candidate in preference to Mr. Thomas Hughes, the author of *Tom Brown's Schooldays*, who had for some time been before the constituency. Hughes, having served in Parliament for several years, would doubtless have made a more useful member than I could be. One reason I was chosen to contest the seat was that he alienated several shopkeepers by championing, with Maurice, Kingsley, Holyoake, and others, the Co-operative movement, which has since made solid progress, and which, I believe, is destined to improve the character, structure, and aspect of civilisation.

The unique satisfaction derived from success at the polling booth was soon marred by a petition lodged by one of the defeated candidates, in which we, the elected members, were accused of bribery, corruption, and other political crimes. We had, in fact, no sooner tasted the joy of triumph fairly won when the cup was threatened to be dashed from our lips. Knowing that every accusation levelled against us was baseless, we prepared for our defence, and in due time the day of hearing came, with Mr. Justice Hawkins and Mr. Justice Pollock as presiding judges. The petitioners' case was opened with a formidable speech by Mr. Digby Seymour. It soon became evident that the charges against us could not, in a single instance, be sustained. On the second day of hearing Mr. Justice Hawkins asked Mr. Seymour "How many more of such miserable rags of evidence he intended to submit." Mr. Seymour pointed to his big brief and pursued the even tenour of his way. But the court got tired of the business, and on the third day Mr. Justice Hawkins said : "Mr. Seymour, would you like to know what I am thinking?" "Yes, my lord," was the reply. "I was thinking," said the judge, "that this trial is costing more than a guinea a minute, which *somebody* will have to pay." The word "somebody" was particularly emphasised. Mr. Seymour, however, declined to accept and act on the significant hint, and the hearing, "like a wounded snake, dragged its slow length along " until the morning of the fourth day, when the petition was dismissed and the petitioner adjudicated to pay all costs on both sides. The hearing might easily have been completed in a third of the time, but, in the interests of counsel, it was irksomely prolonged. Though we, the sitting members, passed unscathed through the ordeal imposed upon us, we had to pay our lawyer's costs to the tune of £500 in *addition* to the taxed costs paid by our opponent! Lawyers generally manage to get the best end of the stick, whoever may be hurt by its use.

I did not find the House of Commons such a fruitful field for usefulness as I expected. It appeared to me that as soon as a majority of members got into Parliament they lost much of the zeal they displayed, in the public interest, on the hustings. However inspired and patriotic they may have been when mingling with their constituents, they took things easy in the House and swam serenely with party streams. Here were gathered together hundreds of men—many, if not most, of whom were well informed on some commercial, legal, social, scientific, colonial, or political question—whose chief duty was to wait about to answer the division-bell and record their votes. It mattered little what was said in debate; in nineteen cases out of twenty members voted on party lines in obedience to party discipline. It appeared as if a goodly number were more inclined to use the House for their own advantage or satisfaction than for the public benefit. There were members who would vote away millions of public money, as if it cost no more to produce than Thames water; members who would defiantly waste the precious time of the House by profitless talk; company-promoters on the look-out for opportunities to extend their City connections; lawyers with an eager eye for professional advancement; scions of the hereditary aristocracy more intent on propping up and perpetuating privilege than benefiting mankind; members who fought for their seats, to use them as stepping-stones to get into "society," or to secure recognition or titles of one kind or another. When a member on one occasion was entering the House, I heard another member say: "Here comes one who is crawling to a peerage." Whether he crawled or not I cannot say, but a few years after he was made "a peer of the realm." The House of Commons is a rich hunting-ground for title-hunters. If the curtain could be lifted so that light might be thrown on the motives and the means used by many to get titles, both the wearers and the things worn would command only insignificant respect. Nevertheless, the House of Commons always contains many able and high-minded men, and might be made the mightiest instrument of general good in the land, if not

in the world. It carries with it a measureless capacity for usefulness, and when all are equally represented by "fit and proper
persons," that influence will be greatly increased. As a rule, rich
and titled men can no more fitly represent working men than
working men can fitly represent the rich and titled. There were
only two working-men representatives in the Parliament of
1880–85. What were two among so many? There ought, at
least, to have been two hundred such representatives; and, if
so, the nation, I believe, would soon be more contented, stronger,
and happier.

Sowing and Reaping.

There is a time for everything; a time to sow, and a time to
reap; a time to gather, and a time to distribute. Having gathered,
I determined to put into act what I had long nurtured in thought,
and use certain means at my disposal for the general good. The
chief question was: How could this be best done to produce the
best result? Should I, in imitation of others, send exploring
expeditions to the North or the South Pole? That appeared too
speculative, and the derivable gains too uncertain. Should I call
into existence new propagandist organisations to promote legislation on liberal lines? That might evoke counter-action on the
part of wealthy Conservatism, now enthroned in privileged
possession, and only to be met and modified by organic action.
Should I provide improved dwellings for the people in London, or
in the form of garden cities? Either scheme was fascinating, but
abandoned, as many others, in different ways, were providing
such accommodation. Should I bequeath funds for public use to
be administered by others? They might not use them as economically as I should. Or should I swim in a sea of luxury like
"the helots of Park Lane," as Sir William Harcourt described
them? That might assist to demoralise others, and probably leave
me morally bankrupt. In all such questionings one idea was
uppermost. As I had accumulated mainly by the labour of others,
I thought, and think, it was only reasonable and just that others
should share in the garnered result; and to act accordingly was a
duty and a privilege—a duty as a citizen and a privilege as a man.
I also thought, and think, that the great working class—the
foundation and bulwark of national existence and the chief producers of national necessities—are entitled to primary consideration in such matters.[1] I consequently decided to do what I could

---

[1] On the occasion of opening the new library and municipal buildings at
Falmouth in May, 1896, I said, in response to a resolution passed: "To the

for their welfare, and thought the best thing to do was to help them to help each other ; and that this could be most productively done by promoting institutional activity. We have hospitals for the sick and wounded, homes for convalescents, orphanages for the fatherless, shelters for the aged, clubs for workers, and public libraries for the many. But all districts have not been supplied, or all pressing wants met. After the best survey I could make of the general situation, I endeavoured to respond to circumstances as they presented themselves, and provide, according to my means, the agency, building, or institution most wanted, and where it was certain or likely to be maintained. Thomas Carlyle says : "Do the duty which is nearest thee, which thou knowest to be a duty. Thy second duty will already become clearer." Yes, a philanthropic spirit is good ; a dutiful spirit is better. Duty is a beneficent mistress. Her teachings and claims are prior to and mightier than the teachings and claims of philanthropy. While a prevailing purpose of philanthropy is to mitigate human ills, a prevailing purpose of duty is to prevent them. There would be little necessity for the exercise of mercy or benevolence if right and justice ruled and regulated human affairs.

VILLAGE INSTITUTIONS.

I began this work in 1889 by building a lecture and reading-room in Blackwater, my native village.[1] That was followed by a

list of toasts on such occasions, which generally included 'The Queen,' 'The Army, Navy, and Volunteers,' 'The Bishops, Clergy, and Ministers of other Denominations,' etc., I would add another—namely, 'The Health and Happiness of our Millions of Working Men and Women.' I hope the time will come, and come soon, when our sense of proportion will be sufficiently cultivated to include in our mutual admirations and congratulations the multitude whose lot it is to labour. When I read an interesting book I long to place it within reachable distance of anyone, however poor and lonely, who would like to read it ; or, when I hear fine music, I say to myself : 'O that the people, the multitudinous people, had the requisite taste and opportunities to enjoy similar satisfaction' ; and as with literature and music so with the other privileges of life."

[1] When opening the Blackwater Institute I said : " Though I have taken part in many such ceremonies, nothing has pleased me more than, if as much as, my visit here to-day. I was born in a humble cottage about two hundred yards from where we now assemble, and the memories of my boyhood clustered and clung around the place ; and, wherever I go or whatever I do, these memories, mostly tender and altogether ineffaceable, go with me. The cottage where I was born, the little school-house where I learnt to read and write, the Wesleyan chapel where I was first a Sunday-school scholar, and afterwards for a short time a Sunday-school teacher, and where on Sunday afternoons I heard so many dull sermons—these places, with the surrounding cottages, fields, and lanes, carry with them an abiding charm ; and your many glad faces, accompanied by the warmth of your welcome to-day, will now be added to my treasured Blackwater recollections."

school and meeting-room at St. Day ; by a literary institute at Chacewater, and afterwards by a miners' and mechanics' institute at St. Agnes—all within three or four miles of Blackwater. One reason why I supplied these buildings was that the villages mentioned were closely interwoven with recollections of boyhood's days and dreams. Distance of time, as well as distance of space, lends enchantment to many views and things. There is scarcely a more unromantic part of Cornwall than the district in which these villages are situated. But, when visited after the absence of half a century, or surveyed through the telescope of memory, they appear mellow tinted. Another reason was that London and other large towns are rapidly growing, at the expense of the provinces and the ultimate strength of the nation. If London, as Cobbett said a hundred years ago, was the " wen of civilisation," what is it now, when it is four or five times as large? And what is it likely to become should it go on increasing, in a similar ratio, for another hundred years? If so, it will more likely carry with it probabilities of national decay than certainties of national advancement. One reason why so many gravitate to the large towns and tread so closely on each other's heels is that village life is generally dull and monotonous ; and one way to make it more attractive would be to multiply village institutions, reading-rooms, clubs, and recreations. This is a question more closely connected with national well-being than is generally supposed, and entitled to more attention than it has hitherto received.

Hospitals.

Physical health is the basis of mental, industrial, and national health, and of moral and material wealth. Without a strong foundation we cannot get, and ought not to expect, a strong superstructure ; and both foundation and superstructure will depend on the health of the units forming the whole. Hospital accommodation assists to repair and build up these units, and thereby promotes both individual and general well-being ; consequently, hospitals have a claim on the sympathy and assistance of healthful people. This would be the case if only physical advantages were derivable from such aid. But hospitals promote the moral as well as the physical health of the people, inasmuch as their existence and action, and the methods adopted to maintain them, are productive of private and collective kindliness. Hospitals are as sacred as churches, and are entitled to as much consideration as churches, if not more ; and nurses are entitled to as much consideration as clergymen, if not more. Many a man and woman, boy and girl, leave hospitals improved in heart as well as health. Many a tender tale and touching anecdote or incident, the result of experience, is told from day to day in humble homes by patients who have undergone hospital treatment. Hospitals, in fact, sweeten the breath and improve the tone of society. Such moral fruitage alone more than compensates for all the means and activity invested in hospital husbandry. Acting under this conviction, I have provided hospital buildings where none existed before—at Falmouth, Liskeard, Willesden, Wood Green, Acton, Tilbury, East Ham, Sutton in Surrey; a new wing, with accommodation for twenty-four beds, to the West Ham Hospital, and a children's wing to the Women's Hospital, Redruth. Four of the hospitals mentioned—those of Willesden, Wood Green, Tilbury, and Acton—have, since their erection, been enlarged and unitedly more than doubled in bed and other accommodation; thus proving that they have not only met local wants and answered their intended purpose in their respective districts, but have sensibly lessened the pressure on the great metropolitan hospitals.

CONVALESCENT HOMES.

Next to the demand for hospitals I learnt that more convalescent home accommodation was necessary. This demand came especially from two quarters—from hospitals and great labour associations. The late Lord Derby, when presiding over the Triennial Festival of the Charing Cross Hospital in 1888, said :— " If a patient in a convalescent stage is kept in the hospital, he is occupying a bed which is wanted for a case of more severe suffering. If, on the other hand, he is sent half recovered to his home, which in many cases is a miserable one, and when the progress of convalescence is slow, much of the good done by the hospital is of no avail." This being so, it occurred to me that in supplying a convalescent home to or for a hospital I was, to that extent, virtually enlarging the hospital itself, or adding to it a new wing— a wing situated amid bluer skies, purer air, and serener surroundings than exist, or can exist, in London or other large towns. I have accordingly provided the convalescent home at Limpsfield for Charing Cross Hospital ; the convalescent home at Cranbrook for the Metropolitan Hospital ; the convalescent home at Perranporth for the Cornwall Royal Infirmary ; the Caxton Convalescent Home for the printing and allied trades ; the convalescent home at Herne Bay for the Friendly Societies ; the convalescent home at Herne Bay for railwaymen ; and the convalescent home for the Workmen's Club and Institute Union at Pegwell Bay, near Ramsgate. It is gratifying to know and to record the fact that, in obedience to my suggestion, the workmen's homes mentioned are under the exclusive trusteeship and direction of workmen.

In proof of the difficulty of securing suitable sites for convalescent homes, and particularly in districts where rich people live in fine houses surrounded with picturesque grounds, I will record an experience in connection with the Charing Cross Home referred to. After the sub-committee appointed for the purpose had visited about twenty obtainable sites, one consisting of many acres near Reigate was selected, for which a preliminary agreement for purchase was made. Certain local gentry, hearing what was proposed, conferred and combined together, brought social pressure on the selling landlord, and prevented the completion of the sale. This may be called Disappointment No. 1. After additional inquiry, the sub-committee next selected a very suitable site, also consisting of many acres, near Sevenoaks. In due course another preliminary agreement was made, and the final negotiation was again defeated in a similar way by a similar combination of rich people. Disappointment No. 2. The sub-committee, so far baffled and beaten, pursued their purpose, and, after more inquiry and delay, pitched on a pre-eminently good site at Limpsfield, near Oxted, in Surrey. In this case also a preliminary arrangement for sale was made; but, strange to say, as if determined by a fiat of fate, a few wealthy people in the Limpsfield district put their heads and their hearts together, and brought sufficient influence to bear on Mr. Leveson-Gower, the selling landlord, effectually to prevent the purchase. Disappointment No. 3.

I mention these facts to show that certain well-to-do people, with full command of the enjoyments of life, entertain an unconquerable objection to their poorer fellow-countrymen and women coming "between the wind and their nobility." Poor men and women are well enough in their places, and particularly when producing the wealth of the wealthy; but they are told, by such acts as I have described, that they must, when seeking health, keep out of sight and hearing of the privileged few, who fare sumptuously every day. It happened that soon after disappointment No. 3 an ideal property for convalescent purposes came into the market; it also happened to be at Limpsfield, and adjoining the property of Mr. Leveson-Gower referred to, and this was submitted for sale at Tokenhouse Yard. It was determined to secure this site, if it could be got at anything like a reasonable price. I had, however, to move with considerable caution, for fear that my object might be suspected and another combination formed to end in another disappointment. I attended the sale, and, fearing I might be known and my intention scented, I sat for two hours on the first seat immediately in front of the auctioneer, without moving or looking to the right or left. The lot, after a spirited bidding, was knocked down to me, and the property was afterwards transferred to the authorities of the Charing Cross Hospital; and on this magnificent site, with its immense stretch of landscape in front, its many hundred acres of public forests behind, and its unsurpassed salubrious surroundings, now stand in triumphant repose the Charing Cross Convalescent Home and the Caxton Convalescent Home.

SAVE THE CHILDREN.

There is another and similar class of work equally entitled to sympathy. I refer to ameliorative institutions for the special benefit of children. The economic and moral waste produced by the neglect, disease, and death of children is incalculable. Better that millions of them were never born than that they should suffer and be subject to the many ills to which they are now liable, and under which they perish early, or become burdens to themselves and society. Of two things one: we should, as a nation, either prevent or at least materially diminish the vast waste of child life in our midst, or say less about our national virtues. We risk much in search of additional dominion abroad, and neglect more promising potential assets in boy or girl life at home. The conditions conducive to such results should be strongly assailed always and everywhere, and particularly in a country which extols its enlightenment, its freedom, its prodigious provisions for national defence, and its imperial destiny. It harmonises with the trend of things that, having promoted organic action for the benefit of men and women, I should act on similar lines for the benefit of children; and it has fallen to my lot to provide one of the Homes for Little Boys at Swanley; a holiday home at Clacton-on-Sea for the Sunday School Union; a home for crippled children at Bournemouth for the Ragged School Union and Shaftesbury Society; a boys' club and institute for the Mansfield Settlement at Camden Town; a home for epileptic boys, and a similar home for epileptic girls, at Chalfont, Buckinghamshire; a children's wing for the Women's Hospital, Redruth; a holiday home for the Sunday School Union at Bournemouth, and the Teachers' Orphanage at Sydenham.

Some two thousand years ago Epictetus said it was better to raise the character of Roman citizens than to add new stories to their buildings. And I venture to say that the best, if not the cheapest, way to improve the quality of citizens, in our age and nation, is to consecrate and concentrate attention on moulding and guiding the young. I remember hearing the late Dr. Farr, an eminent statistician, at a meeting of the British Association, speak on the relative strength of nations. He measured the strength of a nation by the number of men it contained and the proportional number of sovereigns behind each man. He argued as if national capacity and capability of endurance could be weighed by the ton ; and politicians, when discussing estimates, in and out of Parliament, frequently follow a similar line of argument. They are mistaken. National life and character depend mainly on the mental and moral equipment of a nation's men and women. One man, by superior knowledge and experience, may do what two or ten other men could not accomplish. The many are generally influenced and guided by the few. The race is given to the strong. Small nations have produced the greatest and most lasting results. The course of history proclaims the fact that quality has mastered and moulded quantity in human affairs. Where would the British nation be if it depended more on the number than on the ability of its people ? And how can that ability be fully developed and utilised unless each British boy and girl has a fair opportunity for intellectual and moral growth? And who can tell how much our nation has lost by not making better provision for such growth; or who can estimate the rich results which will flow from an ample provision in future ? Thoreau says : " Man's capacity has never been measured, nor are we to judge of what he can do, by any precedent, so little has been done." There is always a rising generation appealing to a risen generation for appropriate and adequate instruction and amusement, and if it gets them it will, in time, show its gratitude in a richer and fuller national life.

PUBLIC LIBRARIES.[1]

When I was a boy I should have jumped with joy if I could have found a corner in a reading-room for an hour or two a day, or have been enabled to take books home as boys and girls can do now where public libraries exist. A majority of people cannot

---

[1] When laying the foundation-stone of the Nunhead Public Library in April, 1896, I said : " I am glad to witness a healthy competition between some parishes in South London in providing public libraries. Man has been called a fighting animal; if so, there was no necessity for him to show his fighting qualities on destructive battlefields. There was no better form of rivalry than that between parishes in their endeavours to distance each other in works of public usefulness. I should like to see another competition—one between men, who had the means, as to who should provide the largest number of useful

say, with Prospero in the *Tempest*, "My library was dukedom large enough." They might, however, and ought to, be able to participate in the advantages of a library created and maintained by public action. As I did a little in the Press in co-operation with William Ewart, the author and chief promoter of the Free Libraries Act in Parliament, it was only fit and proper, forty or fifty years afterwards, when I had means and the disposition, that I should encourage the public library movement. It is regrettable, after so many years and so much general prosperity, that so little, comparatively, has been done to provide such libraries ; and what has been done has, in very many cases, been accomplished in the face of organised opposition—an opposition largely inspired and assisted by the public-house. It is different in the United States. Mr. Choate, their deservedly popular Ambassador in this country, in his address on education at Oxford in August, 1903, said : "At the beginning of the last century there were only twenty-six colleges and universities in the whole of the territory of the United States, and many of these were in an infant and undeveloped state. They are now numbered literally by hundreds, bringing the higher education home to the people everywhere." He also said : "In Massachusetts not even a Carnegie Library is to be found. In that State, which consists of three hundred and fifty townships, all but five have established, each for itself, a free library, open to the use of all citizens, and maintained at the public expense." There are, in fact, almost as many public libraries in a single State in America as we have altogether, after fifty years of effort, in this country ! Mr. Whitelaw Reid, the successor of Mr. Choate, in a speech a few days after his arrival in this country, said : "The city and State of New York spend on free education from taxation funds five times more than was spent in the whole administration of justice." This being so, it is not surprising that the United States should be leaving us behind in the intellectual and industrial race.

Public libraries are, in my opinion, entitled to public support because they are educative, recreative, and useful ; because they bring the products of research and imagination, and the stored

institutions. In most competitions the chief glory consisted of being *first ;* but in such a contest, after having done my best, I should be satisfied to be the *last*. That would be a contest in which the conquered and the conquerors might alike rejoice and be glad. Such a contest would be superior to anything witnessed at Olympian games, where distinguished rivals contended for the laurel crown ; or to anything attempted or achieved on Epsom Downs, where Prime Ministers and aspiring Prime Ministers panted with ambition to win a horse-race."

wisdom of ages and nations, within the easy reach of the poorest citizens; because they distribute without curtailing the intellectual wealth of the world; because they encourage seekers after technical knowledge, and thereby promote industrial improvement; because, being under the public eye, they are economically conducted; because they teach equality of citizenship, and are essentially democratic in spirit and action, inasmuch as they are maintained out of the public rates and subject to public control. All may not use them, but all may do so if they like; and as they are means of instructing and improving some, all are directly or indirectly benefited by them. Nothing, therefore, has given me more satisfaction than to have been able to provide public library buildings at Whitechapel, Shoreditch, Hoxton, Edmonton, Walworth, Hammersmith, East Dulwich, St. George's-in-the-East, Acton, Poplar, Limehouse, Nunhead, East Ham, Plaistow, North Camberwell, Newton Abbot, Truro,[1] Falmouth, Camborne, Redruth, St. Ives, Bodmin, Liskeard, and Launceston.

TECHNICAL EDUCATION.

Moving on parallel lines with public libraries are art galleries, science schools, and technical institutions. Never in the history of the country has there been a time when it was more necessary to foster, by public help, the industrial arts and sciences than now. This is not a mere matter of opinion, but one of certain and commanding importance. Paramount circumstances ask, with united voice, that augmented educational facilities should be placed within the reach of citizens. The strong and well-equipped nation will win in industrial competitions, and its strength and fitness will mainly depend on the quantity and quality of the education received and utilised. The first requisite is the best reachable economic methods of production, and the second is a careful use of the products realised. We have in many ways been following slowly when and where we should have led. Up to

[1] In its report of the opening of the Cornwall Central Technical Schools the *West Briton*, of October 26th, 1899, said: "When Mr. Passmore Edwards was in Truro in April, 1896, on the occasion of his opening the Free Library, of which he was the founder, he used these remarkable words: 'Just imagine a bridge spanning Cornwall from Penzance to Launceston, and imagine, further, the bridge to consist of nineteen big stones, or as many letters as are in my name, and imagine, still further, each stone a public institution, with the Truro Technical Institution as the keystone; such is an ideal bridge, suggested by reality, which I am erecting, and have nearly completed, over Cornwall. Some men have no objection to write their names in characters of blood and fire over war-blasted provinces, or over bombarded and broken cities; but I prefer to write my name, if I write it at all, in characters of light over my native county, and over London, where I have lived and laboured.'"

within the last few years it has been more difficult to get from Parliament a shilling for education than a pound for the Army or Navy. We spent more national treasure—or, rather, wasted it— in the ill-conceived and blunderingly-executed war to crush the Boers than was voted by Parliament for educational purposes during the whole of the last century ! We must now improve our ways and quicken our pace, or lose national vantage-ground. Animated with this conviction, I have, for many years last past, endeavoured to multiply agencies for the extension and application of the arts and sciences ; and to that end I have provided the Art Gallery for the Newlyn Colony of Artists ; the Technical Institute, Hayle ; a similar institution at Helston ; the Art Gallery, Camberwell ; the Central Technical Schools for Cornwall, Truro ; and mainly the Art Gallery, Whitechapel, and the Camberwell Polytechnic.

A COLONY FOR EPILEPTICS.

In January, 1903, I received a letter from Lord Mayor Knill, inviting me to a meeting at the Mansion House to promote the welfare of epileptics. As I had given some attention to the subject, I replied, and said : " I am prepared to present the National Society for the Employment of Epileptics with a suitable farm of not less than a hundred acres, and with buildings convenient for the purpose. I make the offer for several reasons, and among them may be mentioned that such people, smitten with infirmity, are entitled to practical sympathy from their healthier and wealthier fellow-countrymen ; that, as a rule, epileptics are unable to fight the battle of life ; that, being removed from towns, and employed in light and agreeable occupations in garden or farm work, they would, with suitable recreations, improve in health and enjoy existence ; and also because England, with its many advantages, should not be behind Westphalia, or any other nation or province, in shielding and assisting such children of misfortune." The offer was accepted and acted on. After adequate inquiry, and with the co-operation of the newly-formed National Society, I purchased a productive farm of 135 acres at Chalfont St. Peters, a healthful and picturesque part of Buckinghamshire. I have since erected on the farm, which is now called a colony, a house for the accommodation of twenty-four epileptic men, a similar house for epileptic women, a house for the accommodation of the same number of boys, and a similar house for epileptic girls, another house for epileptic men,[1] and a central administrative building.

[1] When Mr. Bayard, the United States Ambassador, laid the foundation-stone of one of the houses for epileptic men at the colony, I said : " One reason

Other houses have since been erected by other generous donors.

It is encouraging to know that this blended moral and industrial enterprise has, from the moment of its inception, made steady and substantial progress, and there is good ground for belief that it will make similar progress for many years. It supplies a conspicuous national want, and carries with it an all-round blessing—a blessing to the hundreds of colonists who work and play there, and a blessing to the community. Epileptics are particularly entitled to practical sympathy, and the best way for their friends, county councils, or poor-law guardians to show that sympathy is to help them to become members of colonies like that at Chalfont, where they can perform agreeable labour in the open air, assist to get their own living, and in so doing promote their physical and mental health; where they can sympathise with each other in their misfortunes, and, in times of emergency, render each other aid, as they do gladly; where they can get and enjoy many of the advantages of home life with prospects of improvement and recovery. Though epilepsy may be classed among brain diseases, epileptics are capable of doing the highest kind of intellectual work. The late Sir Andrew Clark said, at the Guildhall meeting referred to, that " many of the ablest men born into the world, from Sir Isaac Newton to Charles Darwin, were, as children, sickly and unlikely to live. I say the same thing about epileptics. I do not say that Mahomet and Napoleon did much for the good of the world; but they were undoubtedly great men, and each gave to his age ideas which led into new channels of thought. Mahomet and Napoleon, nevertheless, were epileptics."

Other Institutions.

I have been sufficiently fortunate to supply, or to be mainly instrumental in supplying, other institutional buildings which cannot be easily classified with either group before mentioned. They consist of the Museum, West Ham, which has become the home of the Essex Field Club; the Settlement, Tavistock Place,

why I suggested that Mr. Bayard should be invited to perform the ceremony was that I felt sure he would do it to perfection. Another reason was that I desired to utilise ambassadors to promote the pacification of nations. Ambassadors are too frequently regarded as mysterious persons who are much talked about, but rarely seen. If they were seen oftener, and particularly in promoting philanthropic schemes, they would not serve their respective countries less, but humanity more. I therefore would like to see other ambassadors, representing other nations, performing similar acts as they had witnessed with so much satisfaction; and I should also rejoice to see British Ambassadors so employed wherever stationed, and so work harmoniously for the progress of mankind."

with Mrs. Humphry Ward as founder and hon. secretary; the University Hall, Clare Market, the habitation of the School of Economics and Political Science; and the Sailors' Palace, Commercial Road, Limehouse, for the British and Foreign Sailors' Society. These, with the other institutions specified, may be regarded as so many links in the chain of endeavour now being forged by individual, municipal, and Government activity to raise the social life and improve the industrial capacities of the nation. Such forging of links is as interesting as it is necessary; and it is encouraging to know that experience, without an exception, has testified that the institutions it has been my privilege to supply are "one and all" answering their intended purpose and moving in harmony with other organised agencies for general good. And so, in a way, I have realised a triple-tinted dream—first by possessing publications read by many, next by threading such publications with an educating and elevating purpose, and then by devoting industrial gains so obtained to building useful institutions. I may add that I have shown no preference to any creed, party, or connection. I think more of the citizen than the sectarian; more of the nation than any section it may contain; and more of mankind than *any* nation composing it. I have tried to look beyond the particular and the passing to the general and enduring. Individuals die, but nations live; nations and empires pass away, but humanity is immortal. I entertain an idea that every sunbeam that kisses the earth enriches the earth, and that every disinterested act performed by one person for the benefit of another person enriches the performer or receiver, or both, and survives both. The same theory is applicable to all qualities of action, whether it be productive or destructive of good. Like produces like at all times all the world over. An act performed by an individual or a community becomes then and there a part of the unalterable past, and at the same time unites itself with the web of human destiny for ever. If this conception of things be true, what a spacious and inviting prospect encircles every human endeavour which aims at "the best for the most"!

CAMPAIGNS IN CORNWALL.

As I promised to attend most of the founding and opening ceremonies of the public buildings I provided in my native county, I had to economise time carefully when pursuing what the *West Briton* called my "Campaigns in Cornwall." For instance, when opening the Redruth Free Library in May, 1895, Mr. W. D. Bain, J.P., one of the speakers, said: "That was already the fourth time that week that Mr. Edwards had performed stone-laying or opening ceremonies in Cornwall. The first was the laying the memorial stone of the Cottage Hospital at Liskeard; the following day he did similar service for the Newlyn Art Gallery;[1] the following day again he did ditto at Camborne; to-day he opens the Redruth Free Library; and to-morrow he is appointed to perform a similar function for the Truro Free Library." There is a considerable difference in the way such things are done in Cornwall and in London. In London the foundation or memorial stone is in formal language declared to be "well and truly laid." A few short speeches are delivered, votes of thanks given, and all is over in about an hour. First, on such occasions in Cornwall a general half-holiday is conspicuously adopted and enjoyed by all. Then there is a well-organised procession, in which all the town officials and representatives of educational, friendly, and other societies take part; at the ceremony itself several speeches are delivered. Then follows a banquet accompanied by another copious stream of speeches; and, finally, there is sometimes "a carnival," consisting, as it did in Redruth, of music, fireworks, and a procession of allegorical representations.

What Some Sages Say.

In promoting institutional activities I only practised what many of the wisest men of different ages and nations taught. Listen to what some of these sages say! Lord Bacon says: "Seek not proud riches, but such as thou mayest get justly, distribute cheerfully and leave contentedly." Goethe says: "Do not wait for extraordinary opportunities for good actions, but make use of common situations. Hold fast by the present. Every situation—nay, every moment—is of infinite value, as it is representative of eternity." Socrates says: "Employ your time in improving yourselves by other men's writings, so that you may easily get what others laboured hard to obtain; prefer knowledge to

[1] When laying the foundation-stone of the Newlyn Art Gallery I said: "It so happened that, while artists were forming a colony of their own in Cornwall, Cornishmen, in greater proportion to the inhabitants of any English county, were peopling the new colonies of the world. One of my motives in complying with the request made to me to build an Art Gallery in Newlyn was to assist to root these artistic colonists in that locality. Being there, I should like to keep them there. I am, naturally, interested in anything appertaining to the good of Cornwall, and, as the mines of Cornwall were drying up *under* the soil, I am desirous that the world at large should know more of the scenic wealth of Cornwall *on* the soil, and which was scattered in rich abundance within and round their rock-bound coasts. The Newlyn school and colony of artists were illustrating and interpreting that wealth in line and colour on canvas, and thereby benefiting themselves, Cornwall, and the world."

wealth, for the one is transitory and the other is perpetual."
Addison says : "What sculpture is to a block of marble, education
is to the human soul.   The saint, the philosopher, and the hero,
the wise, the good, and great man, may often be hid in the plebeian
which a proper education might have disinterred and brought to
light."   Ernest Renan says : "There is nothing lost ; that which
makes for the good of the most unknown of virtuous men counts
more in the eternal balance than the most insolent triumphs of
error and evil."   Pascal says : "Not only are individuals making
advance in the arts, sciences, and morality, but all mankind are
making continual progress in proportion as the universe grows
older, so that the human race may be considered as one man who
never ceases to live and learn."   Emerson says : "If you tell me
there is always life worth living, that what man has done man can
do, and that man is provided with a key to nature, I am
invigorated, put into genial working temper, and full of goodwill
and gratitude to the cause of causes."   Seneca says : "He that
does good to another man does good to himself, not only in the
consequence, but in the act of doing it, for the consciousness of
well-doing is its own reward."   John Bright says : "Every working man in England is now a ruler of men and a joint ruler of
many nations."   Aristotle says : "Education's noblest end and aim
is to make useful and good citizens, to secure happiness from
worthy lives, to lead to the perfection of man's social nature, and
to encourage deeds which dignify and adorn a country."   James
Martineau says : "What we do for the special benefit of ourselves
perishes with us, but what we disinterestedly do for the benefit of
others exists for ever."   Thomas Carlyle says : "This universe
has its laws.   If we walk according to the law and the Law-maker,
He will befriend us.   If not, not."   Wordsworth says :—

> Thou hast
> Powers that will work for Thee : air, earth, and sky ;
> There is not a breathing of the common wind
> That will forget Thee.   Thou hast great allies ;
> Thy friends are exultations, agonies,
> And love, and man's unconquerable mind.

SOME MINOR MATTERS.

These notes, fragmentary as they are, would be more so if I
omitted to mention a few minor matters which were conceived and
carried out in a similar spirit to the larger ones, and which unitedly
involved as much cost and care as either of the groups of institutions referred to.   I have publicly opened several libraries which I

did not build—namely, the public libraries at Canning Town, Stoke Newington, Barking, Bromley-by-Bow, Tottenham, Walthamstow, the Central Library and Technical Institute at West Ham, Ramsgate, and the library of the Borough Road Polytechnic. In every instance when I have declared a public library opened I have presented it with a thousand or more volumes. I have equipped a boys' reading room at the Cripplegate Institution, and a technical library for the printing and allied trades at St. Bride's Institution. I have also during the last twenty years presented upwards of 80,000 volumes to libraries, reading-rooms, workmen's clubs, schools, hospitals, etc.—varying in number from a hundred volumes to a club to five thousand volumes to the Ocean Library, under the control of the British and Foreign Sailors' Society, Commercial Road, Limehouse. I have added an English Literature Scholarship to the Oxford University; an endowment for free lectures to London public libraries; an endowment for historical teaching at University Hall, Clare Market; a Perpetual Pension for the Printers' Pension Society; a similar pension for the Actors' Benevolent Society; a similar pension for the Oddfellows' fraternity; a public garden for Woolwich,[1] and a life-boat for Broughty Ferry, near Dundee.

IN MEMORIAM.

It is a pleasing duty to place tablets over the doorways of houses in which remarkable men or women were born or may have lived, as the London County Council are now occasionally doing. It is, I think, still more pleasing to place memorial busts of such people, executed by competent artists, in public halls or institutions, as houses, and particularly in London, pass away in obedience to changing circumstances. In the one case we have the record of a fact, which is desirable; in the other case we have not only a similar record, but a *fac simile*, in marble or in bronze, of the head and features of the memorialised man or woman. Such portraits so placed are as interesting as they are instructive, and as commemorative as they are enduring. Hence for many years I have

[1] In December, 1892, in answer to a letter from the Earl of Meath, asking assistance towards the expense incurred in utilising a large unused graveyard of several acres at Woolwich, I said: "I comply with your request. The last thing I would sanction would be the desecration of 'God's acre.' A graveyard, to my mind, is holy ground, and I never knowingly pass one without reverently lifting my hat. But for the sake of the living, and particularly in this overcrowded metropolis, where millions of our poorer fellow-citizens pass more or less comfortless lives, I would make such unused churchyards resting-places for the weary. The object aimed at is so good that, in response to your appeal, I undertake to meet the whole estimated charge, which may be regarded as my New Year's gift to Woolwich."

been privileged to place in town halls, or other public buildings, medallions or busts of famous men or women near where they were born, or where they lived or died. In so doing we gratefully remember illustrious and useful lives into whose labours we have entered, and keep before us examples worthy of admiration. I have placed medallions of Charles Lamb and John Keats in the Public Library, Edmonton; of Sir Henry Austin Layard and Sir William Molesworth in the Public Library, Borough Road; and of Leigh Hunt in the Public Library, Shepherd's Bush. I have also placed marble busts of John Ruskin, G. F. Watts, R.A., Robert Browning, and Elizabeth Barrett Browning in the Camberwell Art Gallery; of William Morris in the Town Hall, Walthamstow; of Hogarth in the Town Hall, Chiswick; of Richardson, the novelist, in St. Bride's Institute; of Elizabeth Fry in the New Municipal Buildings, East Ham; of Emerson, James Martineau, Charles Dickens, Sir Wm. Herschel, Matthew Arnold, and Benjamin Jowett in the Settlement, Tavistock Place; of Richard Trevithick in the Public Library, Camborne; of Adams, the mathematician, in the Public Library, Launceston; of Charles Buller in the Public Library, Liskeard; of William Ewart, the author and promoter of the Public Libraries Act in Parliament, in the Westminster Public Library; of John Milton, Daniel Defoe, John Bunyan, and Oliver Cromwell in the Cripplegate Institute; of George Whitefield in the Tabernacle, Tottenham Court Road; and of Michael Faraday and Joseph Lancaster in the Borough Road Polytechnic. These will be followed by many others entitled to similar commemoration.

Cups of Cold Water.

Drinking-fountains are also entitled to a passing reference. Whether national prosperity ebbs or flows, or whatever party may be in the ascendant, the drink bill, in the face of preaching and teaching, grows more and more; and the publicans manage to enjoy and to exercise a corresponding increase of political power, and that is now always given to one party in the State. Talfourd says :—

'Tis a little thing
To give a cup of water; yet its draught
Of cool refreshment, drained by feverish lips,
May give a thrill of pleasure to the frame
More exquisite than when nectarian juice
Renews the life of joy in happiest hours.

To place drinking-water within reach of many of the poorest, I have, in co-operation with the Metropolitan Drinking Fountains Association and the Metropolitan Public Gardens Association, placed drinking-fountains in Victoria Park; Stalbridge Common, Hackney; The Broadway, Hammersmith; Edgware Road, Kilburn; the Public Gardens, Woolwich; Duncan Terrace, Islington; Christchurch, Blackfriars; Hoxton Square; Leyton Square, Camberwell; Rotherhithe Street, Bermondsey; and Hackney Road Ground, Shoreditch. In constructing these fountains the dog, that faithful friend of man, and destined so often to be cut up alive to satisfy deplorable vivisectionist curiosity, has not been forgotten.

PRESIDENTSHIPS.

In 1881 I was President of the Transvaal Independent Committee, which did much to prevent, at the time, a war between this country and the South African Republic. John Bright one day said to me: "You do what you can outside, and I will do what I can inside the Cabinet, to prevent a war." About twenty years after, I was elected President of the Transvaal Committee, which endeavoured, in the first place, to prevent such a war, and, failing to do so, to mitigate the miseries and shorten the duration of the war waged. That war, on account of the comparative insignificance of its causes, the prodigious inequality of the combatants, with thousands of men and money on the one side, and as many millions of men and money on the other side; and in consequence of the boundless losses, sufferings, devastations, and anxieties produced, will remain a lasting monument of human error. When Lord Rosebery became Prime Minister in 1894, he resigned the presidentship of the London Reform Union, and I was appointed his successor. The Union has done, and continues to do, conspicuous service in the interests of progressive municipal London. It has largely assisted to vitalise and direct collective action on Liberal lines, and to encourage and strengthen the London County Council to make London cleaner, brighter, healthier, and more prosperous. I was also President, for two or three years, of the Anti-Gambling League. Nothing is more certain, and few things more regrettable, than the increase of gambling in our midst. It is seen and felt in most kinds of sport —in the stable-yard, on the racecourse, in the manœuvring conflicts between bulls and bears on 'Change, in schools, in streets, in the homes of the poor, and at after-dinner card-parties in the homes of the rich and well-to-do; and, wherever seen or felt, it morally enfeebles its votaries, whether they be "bookmakers," financial company-promoters, peers, or schoolboys. The gambler is not particular in the quality of his means to secure his ends.

He is ever ready to "make the worse appear the better reason," and to reduce deception to a fine art. The gambler's progress will have to be checked, or he will check the progress of civilisation. Many years before I parted with the *Echo* I decided to sweep betting news out of its columns. I did so in the full expectation that I should thereby sacrifice a portion of its circulation; and so I did of its first midday edition. But what I lost in one way I gained, if not more than gained, in other ways. Soon after I found that the other and bigger editions sold more rather than less in consequence of the change. The change, in fact, raised the character of the paper and conciliated more than it alienated. In similar circumstances I should now, from commercial as well as moral motives, imitate my own example.

A Favourite Footprint.

For more than half a century, or ever since I owned and edited the *Peace Advocate*, the international peace question, with its inviting aspects and promises, has occupied a primary place in my thoughts and affections. No writer who ever put pen to paper could, or can, or will be able to, adequately describe the losses, sufferings, hatreds, horrors, inhumanities, and atrocities of a single great war. A war commenced for one purpose not infrequently originates or developes other blazing issues, which have to be quenched in blood, if quenched at all. Wars, in fact, very rarely settle questions; but they always settle men, and sometimes scores of thousands of men in a single campaign. The costs and losses of a war are generally estimated by the amount of treasure expended and the number of men killed and wounded; but these do not include a half or a quarter of the material and moral damage done on both sides, or a half or a quarter of the heritage of evil entailed on future generations. Well may Mr. Hay, the late American Foreign Secretary, describe war as " the most futile and the most ferocious of human follies." War, in fact, has been the great scourge of the human race. It has decimated the race, bred numberless international suspicions, estrangements, and animosities, and strewn the pathway of history with the wrecks of empires and civilisations. It is the rock of offence against which millions of aspirations have been and are being broken, and by which millions of efforts for human improvement have been and are being neutralised. The chief wonder of future ages will be not that in early times men and women were cannibals, but that in after ages, and particularly when boasting of their Christian enlightenment, they met in organised masses scientifically to slaughter each other.

And what has been done, in soaking the earth's surface with blood and tears by wars, will be repeated unless efficient means are taken to produce a better state of things. What are the means, and who are most likely to use them? The past and present chief wielders of political power in the world, whether they be kings, or emperors, or aristocracies, or plutocracies, or parliaments, have not had the will or the power to prevent wars, or to avoid vast and costly preparations for possible wars, which are almost as crushing and destructive as actual warfare. The same may be said of Churches; and, strange to say, the most greedy nations are Christian nations. But what the classes and Churches could not do or have not done, the masses may accomplish. The common people everywhere suffer most by wars, and can do most to prevent wars, and would be the greatest gainers if wars were prevented. They can make the peace movement popular and powerful by cultivating the peace sentiment in their homes, their workshops, their clubs, their friendly societies, their co-operative combinations and political leagues; by using mediation or arbitration to avoid strikes and settle labour questions; by their votes at municipal and parliamentary elections; by sending greetings on suitable occasions to their fellow workers in other countries, and by welcoming similar greetings in return; and by persistently asking for a permanent High Court of Nations to settle, under the dominion of international law, international disputes. Duelling, or attempt at individual destruction, is, by common consent in this country, regarded and punished as crime, and what one nation like England, with its forty millions of inhabitants, or the United States, with their eighty millions, can do for the benefit of individual citizens, the two nations, or any two or any ten nations, can do collectively for their mutual protection. Substituting reason for violence and judicial methods for war methods, to adjust international questions would make many rough places smooth and unlock undreamed-of possibilities of human progress. I plead for peace and good fellowship among men, not merely as an end in itself, but to urge "man's search to vaster issues." The economic benefits derivable from a peace policy would repay, many times over, any labour or sacrifice employed in producing it; but the economic gain would be small in comparison to the consequent moral harvests that would gladden the world. Happily, a hopeful spirit is abroad and manifesting itself in several countries—and particularly in England, France, the United States, and all the smaller nations of Europe—in the increasing number of international conferences to promote peace, education, science, art, social and political questions; in the multiplication and cheapening of means of inter-communication and transit; in the growing impatience of excessive taxation mainly caused by war expenditure; in the developing solidarity of the labouring classes, and the increasing number of workmen representatives in European parliaments. The removal of the spacious war-cloud that shadows the world would enable peoples to breathe more freely, to work and worship with more gladness, and see glimpses and enjoy foretastes of developed duties and destinies.

GRACIOUS OFFERS.

The following correspondence speaks for itself :—

> 10, Downing Street, Whitehall, S.W.,
> *June 23rd, 1903.*

MY DEAR MR. PASSMORE EDWARDS,—It gives me great pleasure to be able to inform you that the King has graciously signified his intention to confer upon you the honour of Knighthood on the occasion of his birthday.

I must beg of you to treat this communication as confidential until a formal announcement is made on Friday next.

> Yours faithfully,
> ARTHUR JAS. BALFOUR.

> *June 24th, 1903.*

DEAR MR. BALFOUR,—I beg to acknowledge receipt of your letter in which you say that the King has graciously signified his intention to confer on me the honour of Knighthood, and for which I am very thankful. Possibly His Majesty is not aware that the Queen, his mother, offered me a similar distinction many years ago, which, after expressing my gratitude, I humbly declined, and which I again ask leave to do. I nevertheless feel most thankful for His Majesty's kind remembrance of me.

> I remain, yours faithfully,
> J. PASSMORE EDWARDS.

BY THE WAY.

I remember seeing Charles Bradlaugh, many years before he entered Parliament, surrounded and followed by a multitude of men and boys from East London, on their way to a "demonstration" in Hyde Park. Bradlaugh was a very tall man, and wore an ordinary high hat; his followers were short men and boys, who wore low hats of one kind or another, or had no hats to wear. Consequently, the leader looked almost a yard taller than the crowd, and was easily seen. When passing into the Park, I heard one little boy say to another : "There 'e is; let's 'av a shy at 'im." As with Bradlaugh, so it is, I have found, with anyone who may have made himself more or less conspicuous by providing public buildings. "There he is," say a host of the letter-writing, circular-sending fraternity; and postmen soon get more to do and waste-paper baskets get sooner filled. Why should anyone who supplies a public library or a convalescent home be pelted with begging letters to build churches? Or, because he provides a *public* institution, about which he may know much, be appealed to right and left to assist individuals about whom he knows nothing? And the inconvenience is not limited to the reception of begging letters, but includes personal applications; and these, in my case, became so frequent that, contrary to my disposition and desire, I have had to cultivate carefully the habits of a recluse.

Soon after I began to provide buildings for public use I was several times asked whether foundation-stones might be laid with Masonic ceremony. I willingly consented, and, one thing suggesting and leading to another, I found myself, after due preparation and passing well-guarded portals, an "accepted freemason" and member of the Cornish Lodge in London. Experience soon taught me that the conditions of the order were not so exacting as I expected to find them, and were certainly more festive. I will give an illustration. In 1899 the late Sir John Millais, R.A., presided, in the absence of Lord Leighton, who was ill, over the annual Royal Academy banquet. Sir John proposed the toast of the evening, and concluded with a unique eulogium on the president. He said that his noble friend, Lord Leighton, added to his great artistic ability, which all acknowledged, social qualities and administrative ability of a very high order; and with all, if not better than all, he was a very fine fellow. Something of the kind may be said of Freemasonry. It has a noble ritual, wide-embracing sympathies, and useful methods of applying them; and with all, and more pronounced than all, particularly when enjoying "refreshment after labour," masons are "jolly good fellows." The order is limited to no country, creed, or colour, and includes among its members men [no women] of all latitudes and faiths. It is essentially cosmopolitan in character and constitution, and might easily use its broad vantage-ground to promote the solidarity of nations. This could be done by masons at Lodge meetings greeting each other across seas and continents, or by invitations to foreign masons, who may be in London at particular times, to masonic meetings. Such action might, and no doubt would, evoke reciprocative action abroad, and in this way the fraternisation of masons might promote the pacification of mankind.

I have, in more than 9,999 out of every 10,000 days of my life, enjoyed good health, which I attribute mainly to simplicity and regularity of living. During about a dozen of the central and busiest years of my life I was a teetotaler and a vegetarian, and have been mostly so ever since. Man, in physical structure and moral tendency, is vegetarian. Cannibalism has nearly ceased to exist; carnivorosity will follow in due course. The longest-lived and most sagacious animals, such as elephants, are vegetarian. It is the same with birds, such as parrots. Other animals mostly resembling man—such as the monkey tribe—are fruit-eaters. Human flesh-eaters will not, as a rule, eat flesh-eating animals. Where one kind of animal is eaten by man, hundreds of kinds of animals are not eaten. It is more humane to eat without killing than it is to kill to eat. Vegetables, cereals, and fruit can be produced much cheaper and quicker than animals for food. Since I came to live in London its population has more than doubled, and the consumption of bread has increased correspondingly. During the same time the price of bread has materially decreased, and the price of flesh food has materially increased. Fruit and vegetable production is in harmony with the highest human instincts, which cannot be said of cultivating and killing animals for food. Human progress depends much more on what people eat and drink than is generally supposed. Much that goeth into the mouth defileth the man. Many things have recently been said and written about the laws of health and life, and on methods of preserving them; and municipal and government action has been more and more invoked to provide and administer public health regulations. But individuals, by simple living, can do more to protect themselves than can be obtained by the most affluent use of medicine or any amount of legal provision. Indigestion is the mother of many miseries. Modern sumptuous dinners are more akin to barbaric than to civilised centuries, and the fewer they get the better for mankind. Seneca said: "If you are surprised at the number of our maladies, count the number of our cooks."

———

I have more than once been asked, by collectors of facts for biographical dictionaries and other publications, what is my "chief recreation." I have had no particular recreation, as generally understood. I have tried to perform the duties of life with as little friction as possible, and have had a fair share of the pleasures of life. My chief recreation, however, next to reading, has been derived from habitually observing and admiring nature as seen in flower, field, and forest; in billowy landscapes and azurean seas;

or as seen or felt in the pulse of spring and the leafy pomp of summer; in cloud-curtained rising and setting suns; in the exhaustless provision of energy everywhere observable; in the reign of law and the universal balance of things. Nature in essence and operation is recreative, compensative, eternal. It ever waits to impart instruction to seekers after truth and satisfaction to seekers after beauty. Here is a volume with luminous pages open at all seasons to inform and delight its readers, to afford solace to the jaded from overwork or lessons to others who work too little or not at all. The beautiful everywhere invites attention, inspires hope, and offers joy. When a traveller asked Wordsworth's servant to show him her master's study, she answered: "Here is his library; his study is out of doors." All may not have a study or library to call their own, or live within reach of a public library or picture gallery; but most people may, without charge, enter Nature's study, with its grass-carpeted earth, its ebbing and flowing seas, its sunny and starry skies.

––––––

It is surprising to learn from the biographical dictionaries referred to that so many, in search of recreation, should indulge in angling, pigeon and partridge shooting, fox-hunting, hawking, deer-stalking, polo, rabbit-coursing, etc. Such sports must be attended with animal suffering. It is humiliating to know that so many educated people should or could derive enjoyment from wounding and killing, by scientific means, innocent birds and animals; and it is still more humiliating to know that hundreds of thousands of acres of cultivable land should, at the expense of the community, be turned into game preserves and breeding-grounds to provide means for degrading amusements. When a young man, I went with another young man on a shooting expedition. My share of the fun consisted of shooting a sparrow which was enjoying itself on a hayrick. I managed to wound it, when it fluttered down, on broken wing, and took refuge in a hedge near by. Immediately I felt sorrow for what I had done, and carefully searched for the wounded bird to render it assistance if I could, or, if dying, to shorten its misery. But I could not find it. Fortunately I also wounded *myself*. Touched with remorse for my cowardly conduct, I then and there resolved never to indulge in such sport again. I have kept my promise, and shall continue to do so, But that sparrow did not suffer altogether in vain. It was, in fact, a little martyr, and I have since tried to atone for my cruelty by advocating, on suitable occasions, not only kindness, but, what perhaps is better, justice to animals. It may be thought by some that wounding or killing a sparrow is a little thing, and scarcely worthy of a serious thought. Yes, a little thing in comparison to many things, but a great thing to the mutilated sparrow. All things, great or small, are in touch with other things. Justice to animals is inseparably linked with justice to man. The little girl who sends on a postcard kisses to her canary, as well as the Royal Society for the Prevention of Cruelty to Animals, the Humanitarian League, and the Anti-Vivisection Societies, when defending animal rights, are at the same time, and by use of similar motives, promoting *human* good.

Though much has been done, and is being done, in a variety of ways, by individual and combined action, to increase the sum of good, much is also being done in many ways to increase evil. Take two or three conspicuous examples. We see a thousand and one institutions and committees of one kind or another working for social welfare; at the same time, we see Government prodigally spending public money, and thereby impoverishing the nation and increasing the evils such institutions and committees are trying to remove. A still more discouraging state of things may be seen in the wide, and widening, gulf between the very rich and the very poor. We see, on the one side, multitudes of men, women, and children huddled together in hunger, poverty, and dirt; a few hundred yards off may be seen an increasing class revelling in luxurious idleness. We have masses of preventable evil side by side with a section of society who assist to produce that evil by consuming too much and wasting more. London is becoming the metropolis of pleasure, and, at the same time, getting more and more the home and refuge of sweating practices. The poor, by hard and often under-paid work, make the riches and provide the luxuries of the rich; and the rich, by their wasteful habits, largely assist to make the poverty and increase the sufferings of the poor. It is surprising that so many should pride themselves on their independence, their affluent means and sumptuous trappings, when they are dependent on others for everything they eat, drink, parade, waste, and wear. It is equally surprising that the producing many should so quiescently accept such a condition of things. Dean Swift wrote : " I never wonder to see men wicked, but I often wonder to see them not ashamed."

As far back as 1844—I write this sixty-one years after—I met in the street in Liverpool a little blue-eyed girl, with hair like woven sunbeams, who asked me to "buy a brick." In answer to an inquiry, she said they were about to build a new Temperance Hall in Liverpool, and it was supposed that each brick in the building would cost about a penny. Without further entreaty, I bought a brick, and received in return a small picture of a brick on a card. It was the most profitable investment I ever made, as the memory of the incident, and the consciousness that I was joint proprietor, with hundreds of others, of a Liverpool Temperance Hall, have yielded me many pennies' worth of satisfaction. It has since been my good fortune to make other and larger investments of a similar kind, and there is ground for belief—at all events for hope—that the institutions I have been privileged to rear may be so many bricks in the big building of British civilisation.

I Believe.

I believe, with Shakespeare, that a divinity is shaping our ends, rough hew them as we will, and that "Heaven hath a hand in all"; with Schiller, that "Justice is the keystone of the world's wide arch, sustaining and sustained by all"; with Elizabeth Barrett Browning, that "no lily-muffled hum of summer bee but finds some coupling with the spinning stars"; with Herbert Spencer, that "amid the mysteries which become the more mysterious the more they are considered, there will remain the one absolute certainty, that man is ever in presence of an Infinite and Eternal Energy from which all things proceed"; with Mazzini, that "the word Progress, unknown to antiquity, is destined henceforth to be a sacred word to Humanity, as in it is indicated an entire social, political, and religious transformation"; with Thomas Carlyle, "that modern majesty consists in work. What a man can do is his greatest ornament, and he best consults his dignity by doing it"; with Victor Hugo, that "between the government that does evil and the people who accept it there is a certain solidarity"; with Frederic Harrison, that "man's morality towards the lower animals is a vital and, indeed, a fundamental part of his morality towards his fellow-men"; with J. S. Mill, that "we are entering upon an order of things in which justice will be the primary virtue, grounded on equal and sympathetic association, having its root no longer in the interest for self-protection, but in a cultivated sympathy, no one being left out, but an equal measure being extended to all"; with Emerson, that "there will be a new Church founded.........that will have heaven and earth for its beams and rafters, and service for symbol and illustration"; with Humboldt, that "centuries are but seconds in the process of developing humanity"; with Longfellow, that "affection never is wasted : if it enrich not the heart of another, its waters, returning back to the springs, shall fill them full of refreshment"; with Spinoza, "that the good human life lies not in the possession of things which for one man to possess is for the rest to lose, but rather in things which all can possess alike, and where one man's wealth promotes that of his neighbour"; with Ruskin, that "that country is the richest which nourishes the greatest number of noble and happy human beings, and that man is the richest who, having perfected the functions of his own life, has also the widest healthful influence over the lives of others"; and with Tennyson, who "doubts not through the ages one increasing purpose runs, and the thoughts of men are widened with the process of the suns"; and that "the face of death is turned towards the sun of Life."

CONCLUSION.

I have more than once been asked : "What has been the secret of your success?" I have had no particular secret, or any special business ability. I have only taken ordinary care and used common sense. I have, I admit, generally "scorned delights and lived laborious days." I have tried to

> grasp the skirts of happy chance,
> And breast the blows of circumstance.

True commercial success consists in getting means fairly and using them wisely. True political economy is in reality true moral economy. I hate waste anywhere and everywhere. What is wasted by one person is wanted by some other person. The unnecessary luxuries consumed by the few are as detrimental to the consuming few as the judicious use of such means would be beneficial to the few and the many. I would write the words, "Waste not, want not," over the doors of Parliament Houses, palaces, cottages, workshops, and kitchens ; and if the spirit and meaning of the motto were put into practice, the world would spin through space with double joy. While a member of Parliament I always, when opportunity offered, lowered the gas within reach that was burning to waste. I did so for a double reason—to prevent waste and to preserve the purity of the air of the House ; but I never saw or heard of any other member or servant of the House doing a similar thing. I would try to be as careful in the use of public property as if it were my own, and I have been as thoughtful in the use of means for public advantage as in expending means for personal or domestic use.

Domestic extravagance is not the only foe to be feared and

guarded against. Empire ambition, attended as it generally is with additional expenditure, anxiety, and dilution of national energy, should be well bridled and saddled, or it may lead to Empire disaster. A particle of matter cannot be in two places at the same time; as with matter so with men, communities of men, and the spirit that animates them. If individual or national force be expended in one way, it cannot exist to be utilised in any other way. The more a piece of gold is beaten, the wider the area it covers and the flimsier it becomes. As with gold so with national power. That which grows most rapidly is subject to most rapid decay. It is the same with men, mushrooms, oak-trees, and empires. The larger an ambitious and fighting empire is extended, the greater the necessity to protect every part of its frontier as well as its central heart. Certain great nations having entered on an era of industrial competition, the most industrious, economic, and enlightened nation will make the most solid progress, and probably live the longest. What is most wanted at the present time is not a more expanded, but a con-solidated empire, and the best way to consolidate the British Empire is not to fan Imperial ambition, as so many are prone to do and never tire of doing, but to build up at home healthful, educated, and prosperous citizens. By so doing, and only by so doing, can we broaden, deepen, and strengthen the foundations of our commonwealth, make it " four-square to all the winds that blow," and advance human interests by the force of our example. We cannot do this by constantly multiplying Imperial responsi-bilities and anxieties, and at the same time increasing taxation by leaps and bounds, with a large proportion of our people in great towns undergoing physical deterioration. But we can maintain our position and earn national and international fame by a wise use of the industrial and moral resources within reach and under control; by cultivating and applying the arts of peace, and acting towards other nations, great and small, as we would they should act towards us.

———

I must at last bring this hop, skip, and jump record to a con-clusion. I could have said much more about my journalistic experiences; the other papers I have owned and edited; House of Commons life; people I have met; correspondence I have had; complimentary freedoms of boroughs I have received; the associa-tions of which I have been president; the many interesting founda-tion-stone laying and opening ceremonies in which so many distin-guished men and women took part; and the success which has attended the several institutions I have provided; but I have already occupied much more space than I intended, and conclude by repeating what I said in the introductory paragraph, that I have jotted down these reminiscences in the interest of facts and for self-protection, and to prevent, if possible, the publication of inaccuracies in future. On some other and suitable occasion I may supply additional reminiscences to those given, and thereby render the record less scrappy and more complete.

London, August, 1905.

APPENDIX I.

THE following is a list of the Institutions referred to in the preceding pages :—

Public Library, Whitechapel.
Public Library, Kingsland Road, Shoreditch.
The Hospital, Willesden.
The Art Gallery, Camberwell.
The Cottage Hospital, Wood Green.
The Caxton Convalescent Home, Limpsfield, Surrey.
New Wing to Hospital, West Ham.
Public Library, Shepherd's Bush.
Public Library, Pitfield Street, Hoxton.
Home for Little Boys, Swanley.
Technical Library, St. Bride's Institution.
Cottage Hospital, Tilbury.
Public Library, Gordon Road, Nunhead.
Convalescent Home for Charing Cross Hospital, Limpsfield.
Public Library, East Dulwich.
Convalescent Home for Metropolitan Hospital, near Staplehurst.
Colony for the Employment of Epileptics, Chalfont.
Home for Epileptic Men.
Home for Epileptic Women.
Another Home for Epileptic Men.
Home for Epileptic Boys.
Home for Epileptic Girls.
Central Administrative Building for the Colony.
Settlement, Tavistock Place, Bloomsbury.
Hospital and Nurses' Home, Acton.
Public Library, Edmonton.
Home for Crippled Children, Bournemouth.
Polytechnic Institution, Peckham Road, Camberwell.
Workmen's Club and Union Convalescent Home, Pegwell Bay.
Public Library, St. George's-in-the-East.
Enlargement of Hospital, Willesden.
Public Library, Acton.
Public Library, Borough Road, Southwark.
Teachers' Orphanage, Sydenham.
Enlargement of Public Library, Shoreditch.
Convalescent Home for Friendly Societies, Herne Bay.
Holiday Home for Children, Clacton-on-Sea.

Convalescent Home for Railwaymen, Herne Bay.
Public Library, East Ham.
Boys' Club and Institute, Canning Town.
Museum, Romford Road, West Ham.
The Art Gallery, Whitechapel.
Public Library, North Camberwell.
University Hall, Clare Market, Strand.
Hospital, East Ham.
Children's Holiday Home, Bournemouth.
Public Library, Limehouse.
Public Library, Roman Road, Poplar.
Sailors' Palace, Commercial Road, E.
Hospital, Sutton, Surrey.
Public Library, Plaistow.
Public Library, Newton Abbot, Devon.

———

Cornwall Convalescent Home, Perranporth.
School and Meeting House, St. Day, Cornwall.
The Institute, Blackwater, Cornwall.
Miners' and Mechanics' Institute, St. Agnes, Cornwall.
The Literary Institution, Chacewater, Cornwall.
The Technical Institution, Hayle, Cornwall.
The Hospital, Falmouth.
The Free Library, Falmouth.
The Art Gallery, Newlyn, Cornwall.
The Cottage Hospital, Liskeard.
The Free Library, Liskeard.
The Free Library, Camborne.
The Free Library, Redruth.
The Free Library, Truro.
The Free Library, St. Ives, Cornwall.
The Free Library and Technical School, Bodmin.
Children's Wing to Women's Hospital, Redruth.
Science and Art Schools, Helston.
Free Library and Technical School, Launceston.
Central Technical Schools for Cornwall, Truro.

APPENDIX II.

AMONG those who took part in the foundation-stone laying and opening ceremonies of the institutional buildings before mentioned were :—Their Majesties the King and Queen (when the Prince and Princess of Wales); the Prince and Princess of Wales; the Duke and Duchess of York; Princess Louise; the Duke of Connaught; the Duke and Duchess of Fife; Lord Mayor Savory; Lord Rosebery; the Rev. Canon Barnett, Warden of Toynbee Hall; the Duke and Duchess of Devonshire; Sir E. A. Currie; W. R. Cremer, M.P.; the Right Hon. A. J. Balfour; Jos. Howard, M.P.; G. F. Watts, R.A.; Sir Andrew Clark; the Duke of

Westminster; Rev. C. Silvester Horne; Archbishop Benson; Sir James Linton; Dr. Watt Black; the Bishop of Rochester; Sir Thos. Fowell Buxton; Lord Meath; Col. Hughes, M.P.; Lord Mayor Tyler; Major-Gen. Goldsworthy, M.P.; Dr. Wilkinson, Bishop of Truro; Lord Monkswell; Sir Arthur Arnold; Mr. Lowles, M.P.; Sir John Lubbock; Prof. Stuart, M.P.; the Right Hon. G. J. Shaw-Lefevre; Henry Ward, L.C.C.; Sir Walter Besant; Hon. Sydney Holland; the Archdeacon of Essex; F. G. Banbury, M.P.; Lady Burne-Jones; Lord Battersea; Lord Cranbrook; Mrs. Cornwallis and Mr. Cornwallis, M.P.; Sir Henry Irving; Sir Edward Clarke; Sir J. Blundell Maple, M.P.; Lord Chancellor Halsbury; Montefiore Nicholls; Dr. Buzzard; Prof. Ferrier; Sir William Broadbent; Lord Addington; T. F. Bayard, American Ambassador, and Mrs. Bayard; the Duke and Duchess of Marlborough; the Right Hon. John Morley, M.P.; Viscount Peel; Lord and Lady Rothschild; the Bishop of London and Mrs. Creighton; Mr. and Mrs. Humphry Ward; Dr. Richard Garnett; Lord Herschel; Frederic Harrison; the Marquis of Northampton; Sir Edward Poynter, P.R.A.; Hodgson Pratt; the Right Hon. C. T. Ritchie; Lord Chief Justice Russell; the Bishop of Islington; Dr. Herman Adler, the Chief Rabbi; Atherley Jones, M.P.; Sir Henry and Lady Campbell-Bannerman; Dr. Wm. Garnett; Wm. Ambrose, M.P.; Dr. J. S. Brookfield; Lord George Hamilton; Mr. Choate, the American Ambassador; Corrie Grant, M.P.; R. K. Causton, M.P.; Sir Philip Magnus; Geo. Frampton, R.A.; A. E. Fletcher; the Right Hon. Jas. Bryce, M.P.; David Howard, J.P.; Matthew Wallace, J.P.; Adeline Duchess of Bedford; Professor Huxley; the Bishop of Winchester; Dr. Blake Odgers; Lord Mayor Knill; Sir Thomas Roe, M.P.; Mr. Hay, American Ambassador; Lord Leighton; Sir Joshua Fitch; E. J. Nichols; Sir H. H. Fowler, M.P.; Sir Weetman Pearson, M.P.; J. J. Belsey, J.P.; Archdeacon Sinclair; Lord Aberdeen; Sidney Webb, LL.B.; Alderman Bethell, J.P.; McKinnon Wood, Chairman of the London County Council; Lord Amherst; the Right Hon. Herbert Gladstone, M.P.; Sir George Kekewich; Principal Fairbairn; Mrs. Burgwyn; Sir James Crichton-Browne; Sir Benjamin Ward Richardson; Lord St. Levan; the Right Hon. Leonard Courtney, M.P.; Stanhope Forbes, A.R.A.; Archdeacon Cornish; Bedford Bolitho, M.P.; Quiller Couch; Lord Mount Edgcumbe; Cavendish Bentinck, M.P.; Lawson Tait; Dr. Gott, Bishop of Truro; Sir George Smith; R. G. Rows, J.P.; Lord and Lady Tweedmouth; Mrs. Millicent Fawcett; Holman Hunt; Lady Warwick; John Westlake, LL.D.; Lord Kimberley; Sir P. Burne-Jones; J. H. Yoxall, M.P.; J. F. Moulton, M.P.; the Bishop of Stepney; J. Carvell Williams, M.P.; Dr. Newman Hall; Percy Alden, M.A.; Edwin Hain, M.P.; the Bishop of Hereford; Sir Edward Lawrence, M.P.; E. Gray, M.P.; Sir William B. Richmond; Sir Richard Jebb, M.P.; Lord Davey; Dr. Macnamara, M.P.; Anthony Hope; Lady Llangattock; Col. Montefiore; Lord Mayor Green; Lord Mayor Sir Joseph C. Dimsdale, M.P.; Lord Provost of Edinburgh; the Right. Hon. H. H. Asquith, M.P.; Andrew Carnegie; Lord and Lady Carrington;

Viscount Ebrington; Earl Morley; Sir Redvers Buller; Augustine Birrell; Alfred Austin, Poet Laureate; Sir William J. Collins, ex-Chairman London County Council; and recently appointed Mayors of Camberwell, Stepney, Poplar, etc., etc.

APPENDIX III.

THE following are passages taken from some of the speeches delivered at the foundation-stone laying and opening ceremonies before referred to :—

Dr. Wilkinson, Bishop of Truro, when the foundation-stone of the Cornwall Convalescent Home at Perranporth was laid in March, 1891, said he regarded it as an encouraging sign of the times that institutions for the mitigation of physical ailments were increasing, and that no better form of institution could promote that end than a Convalescent Home connected with a hospital, as the one then commenced. They had become accustomed, in one form or another, to munificent bequests; but he considered it a higher and nobler thing, while we were active and had the power and opportunity to spend money in pleasure and the gratification of tastes, to appropriate it to useful purposes, and particularly in lessening sorrow and suffering, as Mr. Passmore Edwards was doing in Cornwall.

At the opening of the Whitechapel Public Library, in October, 1892, Lord Rosebery, who performed the ceremony, descanted on the use of books to individuals and communities. He said the time was come to bring the best books from the central places of learning to the homes and the hearts of the people. The reader, for instance, who enjoys Shakespeare enters a freemasonry to which all the greatest who have lived since Shakespeare belonged. He sits down to a banquet to which no rank, no wealth, without the necessary qualification, or the necessary wedding garment, can obtain admission. Not only by reading is he placed in direct relation with Shakespeare's marvellous mind, but he is placed in communication with all the greatest who have enjoyed Shakespeare's works. We cannot exaggerate the intellectual freemasonry which the cheapening and diffusing of literature has done, and will do, for the people. We owe much to writers like Walter Besant, who had raised a new interest in East London, and we owed equally much to benefactors like Mr. Passmore Edwards, who raised and dignified his gift by the way he gave it. There were no pompous paragraphs, no florid sentences, no blowing of trumpets, or beating of drums. He sent a cheque and a note, in which he said: "I cheerfully comply with your request and relieve you of the difficulty which presses upon you by paying the entire cost of the building. I do this not merely from a sense of duty, but because I think it is a distinguishing privilege to assist in lightening and brightening the lot of our East End fellow-citizens." Acts and language like that find an echo in all hearts, and we know that this is only one of the places he has recently visited in London on a similar mission. In fact, wherever he goes, a suspicion of benevolence dogs his steps.

Mr. G. F. Watts, R.A., put in position the memorial-stone of the South London Art Gallery, in March, 1893. After doing so, he expressed his great satisfaction in co-operating with Mr. Passmore Edwards in the notable work he was doing in London and elsewhere by multiplying facilities for literary and art enlightenment. He hoped that when the hall was erected children would be allowed to come and enjoy its benefits. He had known children of six or seven years of age to appreciate the beautiful in art, and he considered the taste for art could not be developed at too early an age. He was talking a few days ago with a high authority in the literary world, who said that he feared England in the future would be regarded as a second-class nation in a first-class position. Nations that had not developed a real sense of art could not be said to have had a real life. We know little or nothing of some of the great cities of the East, because they had neither art nor literature, while the names of Athens and Florence would last as long as the world endures ; and, with additional educational facilities like the one they were now about to provide for South London, England's achievements in art might, in the future, equal those in other directions.

The Prince of Wales (King Edward VII.), when opening the South London Art Gallery in October, 1893, said : " In my own name allow me to express the great satisfaction it gives me to be present to take part in this ceremony, accompanied as I am by my daughter-in-law and my son (the Duke and Duchess of York), who evince the same interest that I do in the welfare of the working classes. It is a matter of supreme importance that working men should have opportunities of educating themselves by literature and art. They will now have the opportunity of doing so in this magnificent building, built by the generosity of Mr. Passmore Edwards, whose acquaintance I was glad to make to-day, and which we now open. I am glad to think that in connection with this institution many of the workers have taken part in the construction of the building, and I most heartily wish it success, and as heartily thank you for giving me this opportunity of coming to take part in this interesting work."

The Bishop of Rochester (now Archbishop of Canterbury), in thanking the Prince, his son and daughter, said : " They in South London suffered from the fact that, big as they were, consisting of miles and miles of dreary streets, they were comparatively an unknown region to those who could bring sunshine, brightness, and colour into their monotonous lives. But now, thanks to Mr. Passmore Edwards for providing an additional art gallery, to the co-operation of great artists like Mr. Watts, R.A., who the year before laid the foundation of the new building, and others who loaned their art productions for exhibition, they had entered on better days, and the visit of their Royal Highnesses would help to give them the publicity they wanted and the prominence after which they aimed. Few endeavours were worthier than that which they were promoting, and which aimed at raising, brightening, encouraging, and enlivening dreary, toil-stained lives by bringing them in contact with the handiworks of great men, with pictures and other works of art, which would give them something larger, something sunnier, something varied to think about and to admire."

Sir James Linton read and presented an address to the Prince, and said that South London, though covering one-tenth of the Metropolis, contained one-third of its population. The district was cut off by distance and difficulties of travel from the means of intellectual culture in which London, as a whole, was so rich. Within a few years just passed South London, with the exception of the Dulwich Gallery, had no public library, art gallery, or museum. Now the prospect began to brighten, and they were enabled to look forward with hope and confidence to the attainment of rich and extensive results.

When opening the Shoreditch Public Library in October, 1903, the Duke of Devonshire said they had recently witnessed in many directions a great development of the spirit of private benevolence, and an increasing sympathy between man and man and between class and class, and an increased recognition of ties which bound together those whose lot was cast in the same communities and localities. He congratulated Shoreditch on the acquisition of a public library, and he congratulated Mr. Passmore Edwards, its founder and provider. A public library was connected with, and a continuance of, public education. Their object was to raise the material condition of the working class, and to endeavour to get them to make the best use of that material improvement in their general condition. They hoped that education would have the effect of raising, widening, civilising, and brightening the lives of those receiving it. If a larger proportion of those who lived by labour were in the habit of finding their highest relaxation in literature and study, it was more on account of the facilities they possessed of access to books and literature than to any difference in the condition of their lives. Books created in their students a new world and a new life, which was not limited by their surroundings, but was as wide as knowledge itself. The problem was, how this new world was to be opened to the masses of the people—a problem they had assisted to solve in providing the Shoreditch Library.

The Right Hon. A. J. Balfour, on the occasion of opening, in July, 1893, the Willesden Hospital by his sister, said that he and his sister were delighted to take part in an interesting ceremony on an important day in the history of an important part of the metropolitan area. The great growth and concentration of the population of London presented difficulties and problems to everybody interested in the social questions of the day. Legislation could fairly provide good sanitary conditions, proper systems of water supply, drainage, and adequate school accommodation; but legislation could not meet the full necessities of the case. Much is left, and always has been left, and much will continue to be left, to private enterprise when State action ceases to operate. There was no doubt as to the importance of hospital accommodation for the sick poor, which met them with ever-recurring persistence. The existing accommodation was by no means equal to the needs of the central districts of the Metropolis, and still less to those who live in outside districts, where London stretches far away to what, a few years ago, was pure country. One of these districts—Willesden—will now have a hospital of its own. Fortunately, he did not appear in the character of a beggar, as their necessities had been met by the liberality of Mr. Passmore Edwards. "Not in that district alone, or in this kind of institution alone, has his enlightened generosity been called into action. But probably he would not like me to dwell on what he has done in other places and in other cases. I therefore make myself the mouthpiece of this large meeting to convey to him the heartiest thanks for the admirable and sagacious liberality in which he has ministered to our needs."

At a meeting called together and presided over by Lord Mayor Knill at the Mansion House in January, 1893, to promote the establishment of a Colony for the benefit of Epileptics, the late Sir Andrew Clark said that, on inquiry, he ascertained that many of the great men born into the world, from Sir Isaac Newton to Charles Darwin, were, as children, weak and sickly. Although epilepsy was called a cerebral complaint, or disease of the brain, his experience told him that epileptics were capable of performing the best kind of intellectual work. He would not say that Mahomet or Napoleon did much good work for the world, but he would say they were undoubtedly great men, and that each gave to his age ideas that led into new channels of thought. Nevertheless, Mahomet and Napoleon were epileptics.

Sir James Crichton-Browne, at the same meeting, said : When one sees the frivolous crowd at a fashionable resort sickening from want of labour, and the hungry crowd in the East End of London sickening in another way for want of labour ; when one remembers that there are large tracts of the world's surface unsubdued, and tracts in England actually going out of cultivation, in which epileptic colonies might be planted, one sighs for a recrudescence of Carlyleism, that we might again have preached to us the dignity and the obligation of labour. We may accept Carlyle's teaching as to the usefulness and the righteousness of labour, and go further and declare that it is a very valuable and potent hygienic and therapeutic agent, absolutely necessary for the preservation of health, and equally useful in the treatment of disease. The Colony about to be established would be a busy hive of industry, with two sets of products— the fruits of the earth and manufactured articles for sale, and mental contentment and improved health, which are beyond all price.

On the occasion of laying the memorial-stone of a new wing, consisting of twenty-four beds, to the West Ham Hospital, Sir Thomas Fowell Buxton, Chairman of the Hospital, said that for years the population and manufacturing industries of the district had been enormously on the increase, and unfortunately, owing to the nature of the employments chiefly followed, the workpeople were especially liable to accidents; and the result was the accident ward had overflowed and displaced patients from the other wards. The Hospital was thereby rendered altogether inadequate to meet the continually increasing demands of the district. These demands would now be effectually met.

When the Tilbury Hospital was commenced by the ceremonial laying of its first stone in 1895, the Hon. Sydney Holland, Chairman of the Hospital, said that, as a rule, at the best of times the life of the people of the place was uninteresting and monotonous. With the majority of them there was only a week's work between them and poverty; and when any of them met with an accident, or when overtaken by illness, he or she was reduced to the pawnshop. They knew too well in that district what it was to have the breadwinner knocked up or the mother struck down, with no hospital to go to, and without expectation of nursing assistance. Now Mr. Passmore Edwards had made possible what was considered impossible, by undertaking to provide them with a hospital. Now they would be enabled to breathe more freely, and look into the future with more hope; now, should accident or sickness overtake them, they would know where they may go for timely and necessary medical assistance, accompanied by efficient nursing treatment.

The Duchess of Fife, accompanied by the Duke of Fife, opened the new Public Garden at Woolwich in May, 1894. The Duke, in response to a vote of thanks, said that it gave the Duchess and himself the greatest pleasure to be present on that most interesting occasion. Apart from the healing work of hospitals, it was difficult to conceive of anything more useful, more free from abuse, and more full of pleasure, than the work performed by the Metropolitan Gardens Association. It did not pretend to revolutionise the world and make everyone perfect and some people uncomfortable, but it made use of what we already possessed. He thought the amount it spent was little compared with the pleasure it gave to lives which would be otherwise dull; and there were thousands who ought to thank Lord Meath, the president of the Association, and such munificent contributors as Mr. Passmore Edwards, for the amount of enjoyment they had brought into their lives.

On the occasion of laying the foundation-stone of the Workmen's Club and Institute Union at Pegwell Bay, near Ramsgate, in August, 1894, Mr. Hodgson Pratt, the president of the Union, said that between four and five hundred workmen's clubs, with more than 100,000 members, were affiliated with the Union. [Ten years after the numbers were doubled.] The new home which was that day consecrated to public service might be regarded as an institution for the restoration of health and a temple of the modern spirit of brotherhood. It was a source of satisfaction and joy to all to know that to that home, on that beautiful terrace, amid so many inviting surroundings, would, day after day and year after year, come men who had temporarily fallen in the battle of life, for rest and a renewal of strength to be enabled to recommence the battle. The new home would be a blessing in proportion to its use, and that it would be used to its full capacity there was no doubt.

The Right Hon. Leonard Courtney opened, in October, 1895, the Art Gallery at Newlyn, near Penzance, for the general benefit of the public and the special benefit of the Newlyn colony of artists. In declaring the Gallery open, he said Mr. Passmore Edwards had distinguished himself by his gifts in Cornwall, and by the characteristic gift he had presented to that district. The value of the building would mainly depend on the things which were put into it ; and if they wanted to discover the value of their Gallery, they had only to look around, and they might see all the different forms of expression in art, the charm of domestic life, and the magic of local and foreign scenery represented by artists. They might see the beauty of changing seasons, the dreaminess of spring, the pomp and splendour of summer, and the passing away of the strength and the glory of autumn. We all witnessed the aspects of nature from our childhood, but never recognised their full meaning until we saw them illustrated on canvas. We saw the sea every day, the sea in all its moods of calm and storm, of sunshine and cloud, when devastating in wrecks, or when forming an inviting sphere for summer pleasure—all these things were made clearer and more intense when delineated by artists who had shown us what we only half understood before.

Lord St. Levan, who occupied the chair on the occasion, said there was a school of artists known as the Newlyn school. That was a great distinction. They had heard in the days of art of the school of Bologna, the school of Venice, and the school of Milan, and in later years of the great schools of Düsseldorf and Munich ; but he was not aware that it had fallen to the lot of any place in England except Newlyn to give its distinctive name to any school of art.

The Duke of Devonshire opened the first home provided for the benefit of epileptics at Chalfont, Buckinghamshire, in November, 1895. He said : "The peculiar misfortune of those who suffer from epilepsy is that they are debarred, by the nature of their malady, from the remedies most effectual for its cure or mitigation. These remedies are admitted to be regular occupation and social intercourse. There are a large number of occupations which are absolutely barred to this class of sufferers on account of the danger which may be involved to themselves or others through their liability to be suddenly disabled. A large proportion of these sufferers are, therefore, doomed to a life of enforced idleness, which induces a habit of brooding over the unfortunate condition in which they find themselves. On the other hand, it has been ascertained that, under proper supervision and favourable conditions, there is nothing in this infirmity to debar those suffering from it from active, useful occupation; and it has been proved that there is no treatment more effective for the mitigation, or, it may be, the removal, of the disease, than healthy and congenial employment, as that tends to distract their minds from their own individual cases, and to turn their thoughts in happier directions. And now, ladies and gentlemen, I, on my own account and in your name, express our thanks to the munificent benefactor—Mr. Passmore Edwards —who has done so much to enable this establishment to be set on foot."

Lady Burne-Jones, when opening, in December, 1896, the Nunhead Public Library, said that, though they talked of "opening the library," a more important thing was the opening of the books it contained—that silent land of written words by people who had felt or heard or discovered something. She referred to the scheme to found art and technical schools in connection with the South London Art Gallery and Libraries, and maintained that literature and art ought not to be like a magic mirror in which they saw only for a time a vision of what did not exist, and then turned again to an ugly reality. They should be the representation of what they really felt and tried to do in the best moments of their own lives. By worthy lives they could create a worthy art, and everyone could help towards the bettering of art or life, or both, if he would.

The Prince of Wales (King Edward VII.), accompanied by the Princess of Wales and Princess Victoria, when opening the Charing Cross Convalescent Home at Limpsfield, Surrey, in July, 1896, said: "The governors have every reason to be grateful to those whose beneficence has provided this indispensable adjunct to their hospital—a convalescent home—as a resort for patients sufficiently recovered to be no longer invalids and still too incapacitated to be able to work with advantage; and I wish to express my warmest thanks to Mr. Passmore Edwards, who provided the home, and thereby supplied a want long felt. He is also well known to all of you as the munificent founder of the Caxton Convalescent Home, situated in the neighbourhood, and many other similar institutions in other parts of the country. The fresh and invigorating air and the charming scenery will, no doubt, prove an inestimable boon to the inmates of this new institution; and I feel sure that a temporary sojourn here will materially improve their health. We cannot, I think, call to our aid a more valuable auxiliary as a means of increasing the utility of a hospital which, owing to its situation in one of the most crowded parts of London, has no recreation-grounds or gardens. I assure you of my sincere sympathy with the objects of this building, and my gratification at being present on this most interesting occasion."

Mr. Lawson Tait, one of the speakers when the hospital at Liskeard was opened in April, 1896, said the word "charity" was used in two senses —in the Gospel sense of brotherly love, care, and help, and in the vicarious performance of duty—that was, the ticket system—as applied to some hospitals. A man at the head of a factory would give his ten guineas in order that he might have a certain number of tickets with which he supplied his employees who got ill or injured in his service, and for his ten guineas he frequently got fifteen or twenty guineas' worth of hospital accommodation. In Liskeard he was glad to see that they had begun by making their hospital municipal property, and he wished that all hospitals were the same. If they were, many of them would be better managed than they are now, and abuses which now crept in would be avoided.

Sir Henry Irving, when laying the foundation stone of the Dulwich Public Library in September, 1896, said : " This library will give intellectual food and comfort to thousands yet unborn. Its doors will be to many like the portals of an enchanted castle, and the good work which it promises to do will not lightly pass. Let me tell Mr. Passmore Edwards that, in the future, every eager footfall entering on its threshold, and every reluctant one departing, will, in its own way, be the prayer and blessing of a grateful heart. To me, as a player, it is an added pleasure that the building—the dedication of which, to public good, we celebrate to-day—is to be built upon ground given by a player of noble heart for the public good. And I am sure that the trustees of Edward Alleyn's splendid foundation have never, in the course of nearly three centuries, exercised their power of trust in a way which would have better pleased the founder than when they gave over the ground for the uses of this Library. To-day this act sheds a new lustre upon a name which all must love and respect, and adds a new honour to the man and a new dignity to his calling. Here we have a great union, land given by a player—the friend of Shakespeare—whose art life was devoted to the encouragement of the imagination, and a building won by the literary work and enterprise of Mr. Passmore Edwards. Alleyn's noble foundation was so sweetly named the College of God's Gift ; so may the later manifestation of whole-hearted public spirit and true charity be ever followed by God's blessing."

Lord Chancellor Halsbury publicly declared, in the presence of a large gathering of listeners, the East Dulwich Public Library open in November, 1897. He congratulated Camberwell on having made so much progress in developing one of the most favourable features of the present era of civilisation—he meant the establishment of free public libraries. When he looked around on the one they were then opening, which was magnificent in more senses than one, he supposed that no college or university two or three centuries ago could boast of such a collection of the thoughts of great men. There was nothing more delightful than a library, and people who possessed them could realise how valuable they were and how much they are enjoyed by less fortunate persons. Some people complained of the large number of fiction-readers who used public libraries. That might apply to some ; but he maintained that the imagination as well as the memory should be cultivated. John Milton said that a man might drown himself in books and yet be very shallow ; but that remark only applied to the abuse of books. There was good reason to believe that the library

G

then commenced would be a great boon to the people of Camberwell, who expressed their gratitude to Mr. Passmore Edwards for making its realisation possible.

———

Lord Monkswell, on the occasion of laying the foundation-stone of the Kingsland Road Library, Shoreditch, in June, 1896, said it was his privilege, as senior member for that district on the London County Council, to move a vote of thanks to the donor. It was not unusual for persons to give large sums of money, to come into operation after their death. But Mr. Passmore Edwards distributed his gifts during his lifetime, and saw with his own eyes the splendid benefits these gifts bestowed on the country. He not only provided the means, but took a personal interest in the birth and growth of libraries and the other useful institutions he successfully founded. He did this by conferring with committees, architects, builders, and librarians, so that the means at his disposal might be economically administered and the greatest good for the greatest numbers secured. He (Lord Monkswell) felt confident that in that industrial centre thousands of persons would have their lives brightened and their faculties and powers of enjoyment increased by the magnificent action of Mr. Passmore Edwards, whose name would not only be inscribed on the Haggerston Library, but within the minds and hearts of the people.

Early in 1897 Sir Arthur Arnold opened the enlarged Public Library in Kingsland Road, Shoreditch. He said the march of intelligence, acted on so powerfully by public libraries, had done and was doing much for the endowment of London with that ennobling sense of community which was a new experience in their gigantic capital. Whether reading became serious or frivolous depended very much on the character and object of the reader. There was a great difference between the pursuit of knowledge and the acquirement of wisdom. "Knowledge dwells in minds replete with the thoughts of others, wisdom in minds attentive to their own." Literature had votaries of every class and order of mind ; but those who read and studied in a pure and trusting spirit would never find themselves forsaken or disconsolate. He obeyed with alacrity the invitation to open the extended building, partly because of the position he held as head of the central government of London, and partly because he thought he could do no better service to the citizens of London than thus to acknowledge the benefaction of which his old and honoured friend Mr. Passmore Edwards was the donor.

———

Mrs. Humphry Ward laid the foundation-stone of the Edmonton Public Library in April, 1897. She said : "When we have all passed away generations of English people, in and around London, and in the remote towns of beautiful Cornwall, where Mr. Passmore Edwards has erected so many public libraries, will still be entering the spiritual kingdom of knowledge and imagination, so opened up and widened. Free libraries are the great opportunities of our day and the days to come. Perhaps the majority of those who come to them will come for pleasure and rest, and small blame to them, for our modern life is a hard and hurrying one.

Perhaps, through the library, the commencement of which they had just witnessed, some Edmonton boy in the future, gifted beyond his fellows, will produce a poem, a novel, or a history which will stir new and fruitful ideas in the English mind. There is always that chance, which should never be neglected or discouraged, because certain clever people, who had all the advantages that the endowments of the English higher education can give, throw a little mud at free libraries. Youth is the time for reading and study, as it is the time for that public and complete joy realised in the world of literature. Their whole after life might be the richer for it, whether in their daily work or in business or in colonising—that great indispensable work of pushing forward and spreading the British Empire, which, unless we can infuse into it a higher temper, a temper of justice and mercy, will more likely lead to national sorrow than national honour. We depend for the solution of our national difficulties, far more than most of us imagine, upon the humanising of English feeling and imagination, and it was in public libraries they will find the means of nurture and improvement."

Lord Rosebery, after declaring the Shepherd's Bush Public Library open, in June, 1896, said that, when he was in office and subject to all the responsibilities and censures of office, he found time in the very beginning of that period to go and open a library, founded, of course, and given, of course, by Mr. Passmore Edwards. He (the noble lord) went on to say that those who watched the progress of the nation had some cause to inquire what object the public libraries fulfilled in modern economy. No one could watch the course of events without seeing the great predominance given everywhere to outdoor sports. He welcomed that tendency; it was healthy and rational, but might be carried too far. We had to maintain a great Empire, and for Imperial purposes we needed a race of muscle and nerve which were developed by such sports. The Empire, however, could not live by muscle alone; it must have brains, and to have brains we must have the requisite educational appliances. Primary and secondary education would do much, but they would not give us all we required. What we wanted to develop in our race was the art of thinking—an art which stood a good chance of perishing among us. The risks to which independent thinking was exposed were manifold and dangerous. The mind of England, which was the most receptive mind in the world, was beginning to be deadened to external impressions, and he feared that intellectual apathy was the great danger of the nation; and he hoped and believed that public libraries would be a counteraction to that apathy.

Dr. Richard Garnett, of the British Museum, when opening the Edmonton Library, said: "The mass of our people have more of the rights, duties, and responsibilities of citizenship than formerly, and they are exposed, as never before, to the competition of active, intelligent, and, in general, well-educated rivals. The great extension of the means of communication by railway and telegraph has made every part of the world virtually next-door neighbour to every other part.   Events in remote countries affect us far more intimately than was formerly the case. We are obliged to go afield to push our commerce, and wherever we go we find that one chief obstacle is our ignorance, confronted with rivals better informed than ourselves.   Wide miscellaneous knowledge is requisite, but such knowledge cannot be obtained at school   All the school can do is to hand the pupil on to the library, where, if he rightly imbibes the spirit of the institution, he will find himself entering upon a new development of education—self-education—never to end but with his life ; and where, if he cannot acquaint himself with all topics, he will at least find himself in contact with a magazine of information ready to be applied to every emergency, public or private, as it may arise."

On May 9th, 1897, Mr. Bayard, the American Ambassador, laid the foundation-stone of one of the homes for epileptic men ; and on the same occasion Mrs. Bayard opened the Home for Epileptic Women, at Chalfont St. Peter's, Buckinghamshire.   Mr. Bayard said he could not express the gratification he felt that, on the close of four years of service as the Envoy of the United States, he should be privileged to speak to such an assembly on such an occasion.   It was intended to make that colony a centre of health and an organised promoter of industry.   Those who came there would be employed in some useful way, instructing their minds and bodies, so that each should react on the other.   Just as there was an equilibrium of the body and its vital forces, so there was an equilibrium of the body politic and the social forces ; and it was all-important that the healthful flow of youthful interest and mutual sympathy should pervade all classes.   The fate of one influenced the fate of all, and the interests of all were common interests ; and he knew of nothing which keeps alive so much as the exertions so nobly illustrated by the life and career of Mr. Passmore Edwards, the founder of that colony, whose discriminating benevolence was so well worthy of imitation.

The following is an extract from the 1897 Report of the Society for Employment of Epileptics : "When we reflect upon all that has been accomplished, not only for our own, but also for so many other public and charitable undertakings, by the unfailing liberality of this truly illustrious benefactor, we cannot but feel deeply impressed, not only by the direct results achieved through his munificence, but also by the conspicuous example which he has set to the wealthy of his own and succeeding generations—an example which will, we believe, have a vast influence in stimulating and perpetuating those principles of voluntary effort upon which in this country movements for the benefit of the poor and the afflicted are so largely and so wisely based.   Throughout the length and breadth of the land may be found structures raised at the bidding of Mr. Passmore Edwards for the welfare of the people and the succour of the weak and suffering.   Many a stately edifice will testify to coming generations his goodness and his fame ; yet well might the builder of these material monuments lay claim to a memorial loftier and more lasting still."

The Right Hon. C. T. Ritchie, when fixing the memorial-stone of the Public Library in St. George's-in-the-East, in 1897, said that in his former Parliamentary connection with the borough he had frequent occasion to deplore the great scarcity, he might say the total absence, of places for study and recreation. They had constant evidence of the good such institutions were doing in other places. That condition of things would now be mitigated by the magnificent generosity of his friend, Mr. Passmore Edwards. He had no doubt the library, when in working order, would prove a public blessing. The lady librarian of the People's Palace could tell them that she saw, year by year, a marked improvement on the part of readers in their desire for increased *useful* knowledge. As might be expected, the books most inquired for, and most read, were works of fiction. He confessed to a strong sympathy in that direction, as he found nothing more enjoyable than a good lazy day and a three-volume. novel. The same lady librarian informed him that, next to novels, the books most in request were those on technical and practical subjects, which was strong evidence of the value of public libraries.

Lord Chief Justice Russell opened the St. George's-in-the-East Library in October, 1898, and said that free libraries carried with them many advantages, and among them a counter-attraction to many evils. Many poor people were attracted from their cheerless homes to the snug and well-lighted rooms of the public-house, and it was important that they should have opportunities to spend their leisure time with profit. There was a time when Great Britain had no rivals; now, rivals were appearing in most directions. England could not hold her place unless her artisans were properly educated; and no one had done more to secure that end than Mr. Passmore Edwards. A characteristic of his work was that he was displaying no posthumous munificence—a strong contrast to the action of many who disposed of their wealth for philanthropic purposes when they could no longer hold it in their own hands. Mr. Edwards needed no commendation from him, neither did he require a monument. All over the country it could be said of him, *Si monumentum requiris, circumspice.*

Dr. Herman Adler, the Chief Rabbi, in moving a vote of thanks, spoke of the admirable work Mr. Edwards was doing, and particularly in East London, by bringing within reach of the poor the fruits and flowers of literature, and by enthroning them in such a beautiful building as the one in which they were assembled. The poorest may now come and feel themselves at home in this new garden of delights provided for their instruction and entertainment. They may come and cultivate the companionship of books, hold communion with illustrious thinkers and teachers, and by so doing improve and brighten their lives.

When the Princess Louise opened the Convalescent Home at Cranbrook, Kent, in July, 1897, Lord Battersea responded to a vote of thanks to Her Royal Highness, and said the Home would provide accommodation for eighteen convalescents from the Metropolitan Hospital, which was situated in one of the poorest parts of London, and surrounded by thousands of houses closely packed together. Sailors who were injured in the docks, and others who came home sick from foreign service, besides large numbers of the poor of the district, found medical assistance at the hospital. It was essential that some patients in the hospital, before returning to their work, should spend some time in a convalescent home, which they had long wanted; and now Mr. Passmore Edwards had generously leapt into the breach and provided the home, with Mr. Cornwallis giving the site. The hospital and the home would go hand in hand, and many would have an opportunity of receiving convalescent advantages in addition to medical and nursing aid; and Her Royal Highness, by opening the home, would be enabled to add another remembrance similar to the many she cherishes by bestowing her smile on another deserving institution. ————

When Lady Rothschild laid the principal stone of the Acton Cottage Hospital, in June, 1897, Lord Rothschild, in reply to a vote of thanks to her ladyship, said Mr. Edwards, in providing the hospital, presented to the parish a precious gift, not only in the building he was erecting, but in his call on the people of the district to maintain and make it flourish. In that the charity would be more precious and more beneficial to all concerned than if Mr. Edwards had endowed it and left it to languish in the hands of trustees.

The Bishop of London (Dr. Creighton) opened the Acton Hospital and the Nurses' Home in May, 1898. The Bishop said the growth of civilisation depended not on the growth of what we individually possessed, but upon the growth of what we possessed collectively; and it was most necessary that the collective provisions for the public good should cover, above all things, those times of life when we most feel the need of assistance from others. Such a time was a time of sickness. It was at such times we especially felt our dependence on others, and how our lives were knit up with others. What a great thing it was for the poor people of Acton to be able to look upon that building and say: "Well, there is one comfort: if I am taken ill, I know where I may go and be looked after, and where I shall receive all the attention and help the wealthiest man can command with his money." He therefore, in the name of the people of the district, told Mr. Passmore Edwards how deep was their debt of gratitude to him, and that they hoped the hospital, by its increased beneficence and constant activity and the use made of it, would carry his name to the generations yet to be, and tell how, in the year of the Jubilee, they were enabled to enter on a new possession that made life more valuable to all who lived within the reach of its influence. ————

Sir Edward Poynter, when opening the Camberwell Technical Institute in January, 1898, said it was a matter of rejoicing that the building should, at the suggestion of the donor, Mr. Passmore Edwards, be dedicated to the memory of Lord Leighton, who stood so high among English painters as an artist in the real sense of the word, and as one having complete mastery of his craft, as opposed to that fatal amateur element which was so frequently seen in our artists and craftsmen.

Schools of art might be of the greatest value if their proper purposes were kept in view, and if it were remembered that a *dilettante* admiration for old art and an enthusiastic talk about beauty of form and feeling in colour went for nothing, that dabbling in wood-carving and pottery did not make a workman, and that even originality in design was only half the battle. We had in this country designs enough and to spare. What we wanted was fine craftsmen, who would put their best work into all they did for the love of it. If the example of great artists and the fine works of art of past times were to be of any value, they must be studied not with a view to mere imitation of style, but to the perfection of workmanship displayed in them, and which was to be gained only by years of apprenticeship under good traditions. The name of Lord Leighton ought to be an incentive to use the Camberwell Institution in the only direction in which it could be of real value.

Viscount Peel, after laying the foundation-stone of the Whitechapel Art Gallery in December, 1898, with many other good things, said it was permissible, standing as they were in the cradle of a new building, to take an interest in its future life and speculate on what might be its fortune hereafter; and he thought he was justified in prophesying that it would for years and generations be a place where intelligent recreation would be obtained, and where the minds, hearts, and imaginations of many of the toiling population of East London would find solace, improvement, and happiness. That pictures elevated they had proof everywhere. He pictured a possible future in the realms of art, when great portrait painters might be found who "behind the mask of the human face would see the inner soul," and when great landscape painters "will see nature through the medium of their own intense and loving imaginations," and unlock the secrets of nature in such a way as no photography could possibly represent.

The Right Hon. John Morley opened the Settlement in Tavistock Place, Bloomsbury, in July, 1898. The following are the opening sentences of his elaborate speech on the occasion :—" I am extremely glad to have an opportunity of paying a tribute to the munificence and public spirit of Mr. Passmore Edwards—a munificence not only in this beautiful building in which we find ourselves, but, I think, in no fewer than sixty other edifices [since then many more], all contributing, as he would describe his own purpose and view to be, to the stream of individual and organised endeavour in spreading light for those who are whole, and doing something to ameliorate the lot of those who are stricken and sick. He has not only been generous, but has exercised his generosity with discriminating care among the various competing objects of his bounty. It is a splendid example of generosity, which I hope will provoke a spirit of noble emulation and find many imitators. I understand that if London were properly provided with settlements, and similar institutions, you ought to have one in every 20,000 of the population, and, therefore, there is an abundant field for emulating the example which has been so worthily set. There are others who have contributed to this work without stint of valuable time, thought, and zealous interest, which is really more precious than silver or gold ; and we certainly cannot pass over that lady of so many gifts, who is regarded as the foundress of this particular settlement, and who has shown how deeply she has felt the truth that

> Fame with men
> Brings but ampler means to serve mankind.

These words of Tennyson exactly describe, I take it, the spirit in which Mrs. Humphry Ward has won the laurels which have been so deservedly placed upon her brow. Mrs. Ward, by personal service, has made the way easier both for men and women who intend to devote themselves in her spirit, to the same ends, which she has made so familiar and so cherished. I cannot but note a new mark of our time, and Mrs. Ward reminds me of it."

The Marquis of Northampton, when commending the "Home for Cripples," at Bournemouth, on its mission of usefulness in June, 1898, said the Home could not fail to be serviceable, as many cripples would, by its assistance, be strengthened or completely restored. Cases had occurred in some of the Ragged School Union Homes of children who had come helpless and returned home able to walk ; and all, whether their stay at the Homes were short or lengthened, were more or less benefited. The Bournemouth Home was intended to be a home in the best sense of the word. Under the doctor's advice the little ones would have good air, shelter, care, protection, healthful and agreeable recreation, and a six months' stay with a view of their permanent benefit.

Mr. A. E. Fletcher, who unveiled the memorial medallion of Leigh Hunt at the Shepherd's Bush Public Library, said : "Let us remember Shelley's fine description of Leigh Hunt as 'one of the happy souls who are the salt of the earth.' We have learnt enough to admire him for his genius and his marvellous industry, to honour him for his fearless outspokenness and courageous sacrifice for principle, and to love him for his splendid faith in humanity and his buoyant optimism. The silly slander that a certain contemptible character in *Bleak House* was intended by Dickens for a portraiture of Leigh Hunt was indignantly repudiated by Dickens himself. Hammersmith had reason to be proud that such a man dwelt within its borders, walked its streets, and looked with a poet's eye upon the sunsets of its noble river, and it was highly creditable to Mr. Passmore Edwards' qualities of head and heart that he should first present Hammersmith with a splendid public library, and then adorn the walls of the library with a commemorative medallion to Leigh Hunt."

Professor Stuart, M.P., on the occasion of laying the first stone of the Hoxton Public Library in June, 1896, said, as member for the division in Parliament, he was pleased to move a vote of thanks to Mr. Passmore

Edwards, not only on account of his action on that day, which was but a sign and seal of other matters, but because of his great generosity in the parish. They owed their two libraries to his action, and his name in connection with public libraries and many other forms of public munificence had become well known; and his generosity was aptly illustrated in connection with public libraries in the great position he had long occupied in the public Press, a position he had made by dealing with a high class of literary production.

The Right Hon. G. J. Shaw-Lefevre, who followed, said Mr. Edwards in the Press had set before himself a high ideal, and harmonised his actions thereto; and he was now devoting a large proportion of what he had so well earned to the public good.

Sir John Lubbock, when opening the Hoxton Public Library in April, 1898, said they had been somewhat slow in London in availing themselves of the advantages of the Public Library Act, as, during the first sixteen years, only one such library had been opened in the Metropolis, and Westminster had the honour of taking the lead. In the next ten years not a single public library was started in London, and from 1877 to 1886 only two were opened. But, from that time, a new impulse had manifested itself, and London could now boast of forty public libraries, for fourteen of which they were already indebted to the wise generosity of Mr. Passmore Edwards, who had provided many more in Cornwall. They were beginning to realise that education was not merely a matter of schools and children, but that it goes on through life. Free libraries were really continuation schools and universities, doing an enormous amount towards the technical and general progress of the people. A library was a new fairyland, a very palace of delight, a haven of repose, where amusement, comfort, and consolation would be found by everyone who brought to it the right frame of mind; and he felt confident that the one he then declared open would add, in many ways, to the enlightenment and prosperity of the district.

Mr. McKinnon Wood, Chairman of the London County Council at the time, after adjusting the first stone of the Public Library, East Ham, in November, 1898, said that with some books it was only worth while to have merely a bowing acquaintance, there were some that would repay a more intimate knowledge, while others were worth making enduring friends. Some people use books to show their culture and refinement, as ladies use flowers to decorate a room. Good books had in them a vitalising potency. John Milton said: "A good book is the precious life-blood of a master spirit, embalmed and treasured up on purpose to a life beyond life." The hundred best books for one person would not be the best books for another, as the minds of men resembled different soils. Here the gardener would plant flowers, and there an orchard. If a book left the mind thinking, it served its highest office. Books must be cultivated as friends, and they then opened their souls to their readers.

When Mr. Frederic Harrison unveiled two medallion portraits, executed by Mr. George Frampton, R.A., at the Edmonton Public Library, he said: "In offering to this fine Library and Institution, in which we meet to-day, the medallion portraits in bronze of Charles Lamb and John Keats, the founder has still further enlarged his noble gift, and added to the people of Edmonton a new claim to their grateful acknowledgments. This handsome foundation is one of scores of others which will long record to our descendants the name of Passmore Edwards. These nurseries of thought and culture are the munificent gifts to his fellow-citizens of one who is a member of the literary order and the founder of a new era in journalism. It is an example of public spirit far more common in the United States than in Europe. In England our magnates of rank and vast possessions think they can best gratify public tastes by admitting people to view their galleries or their race-horses. The wealthy citizens of America are more given to devote their abundance to the public, and have given a large share of the universities, libraries, observatories, and museums to the States. Most of the immortal dramas of Athens, and many of the remains of Greek architecture which we see to-day, were the free gifts to their fellow-citizens of rich and patriotic patrons, such as Herodes Atticus in the time of the Empire. The example is too rare in England—almost unknown in London. Let us hope that in the course of time the South of England and its capital may receive such real benefactions as are common in America, and not unknown to our northern counties, and that London, too, may count its Passmore Edwards, and follow the example of the Herodes Attici of old."

The Right Hon. Sir H. H. Fowler, M.P., in May, 1898, laid the foundation-stone of the Sunday School Union Holiday Home at Clacton-on-Sea, and said there was no agency in the previous history of the world which could compare with the Sunday-school movement and the good work it had done by voluntary labour alone. Difficulties such as "conscience clauses" and other controversial matters vanished in the presence of the Sunday-school system. One commanding feature of that system was the sending of children for the enjoyment of holidays into the country or to the seaside. Dr. Arnold, of Rugby, objected to teach a boy who had not seen the sea, because the sea enlarged the boy's mental horizon, and made him an apter scholar. For many years the Sunday School Union had utilised some of its thought and means by sending children to pleasant country and seaside places; and now, thanks to Mr. Passmore Edwards, they would carry on their work on a more extended scale. It was difficult to speak of Mr. Edwards and the marvellous conception of philanthropic generosity he had grasped, and which he had the power and the will to carry out.

Lord Aberdeen, on the occasion of opening this Holiday Home in June, 1899, said the name of Mr. Passmore Edwards had not only become familiar, but had become a household word, and was cherished with admiration and gratitude. He congratulated him not only for his great philanthropic work, but upon his discrimination, prudence, and foresight. In his connection with the Press he imparted a high tone to journalism in the newspaper enterprises under his control; and in the Clacton Home they had additional evidence of his qualities of head and heart. Holidays were a necessity, but hitherto they had been but little enjoyed for want of the necessary provision; now, hundreds and thousands, in the years to come, would find in and around the one opened that day sources of health and enjoyment.

The Venerable Archdeacon Sinclair preached a dedicatory sermon in the Clacton-on-Sea Church the day before the opening of the new Holiday Home. He said it was a sad thing to think of the boys and girls of London cooped up all the year round in hundreds of thousands in houses in dull and dusty streets, where the sky is usually grey with a canopy of smoke and with fields and flowers far away. And of all the great and useful charities with which the name of Passmore Edwards will be held in lasting honour and remembrance as founder, not one, he thought, would bring more happiness to him than the Holiday Home for the children of our Sunday schools at Clacton-on-Sea.

When Lord George Hamilton, Minister for India, laid, in 1898, the first stone of the Acton Public Library, he said he had many opportunities, and particularly in the Midland Counties, of judging, and could not fail to conclude that a public library was an enormous advantage to the locality in which it was situated. It offered means of self-education and improvement to thousands of young men whose opportunities for such improvement were prematurely cut short by the necessity of earning their livelihood; it was an antidote to those places of public resort where people too frequently contracted deleterious habits; and it discharged a public service by becoming a ready centre of knowledge where those who took an interest in public affairs could acquire the latest and most accurate information. He learnt that after the establishment of a public library greater interest was taken by the people of the district in public questions. A limit of a penny in the pound was a great obstacle to obtaining a library in many places, and, unless a benefactor had come forward, they would have had to wait many years in Acton before they had a library suitable to their wants. Such a benefactor was Mr. Passmore Edwards. He congratulated that gentleman on the magnificence of his benefactions and the principle of action which guided him in their distribution. He made no parade or show. What he did was to find the wants of a district, and then provide the requisite assistance on condition that the institution must be maintained when placed on its legs.

Mr. Choate, the American Ambassador, opened the Acton Library in January, 1890, and said if there was one thing in which Americans of all creeds, parties, colours, and social conditions were heartily agreed it was upon the subject of education, and of free libraries as a necessary part of education. The American common school system, dating back to the earliest days of colonial life, provided education at the public expense for every boy and girl up to years of discretion; and public and private munificence supplemented that system of education by the establishment of free libraries, and thus bringing knowledge home to the very doors of the people throughout the land. Their free libraries were numbered by thousands ; every considerable town was proud of its library, and towns were graded and measured according to the dignity and usefulness of the libraries they possessed. So urgent were the authorities to bring easy access of knowledge home to the people, that in New York and some other large towns a regular system of travelling libraries had been established, in addition to the stationary libraries ; and 100 volumes made a regular tour through the remote districts, and were followed at intervals by similar collections for exchanges. London had the greatest and noblest library in the world—the British Museum Library ; and now there was a necessity which had been recognised (and Mr. Passmore Edwards was a pioneer in recognising it) for the establishment of *local* libraries—libraries which would come home, as justice should come home, to the universal people.

———

The Right Hon. James Bryce opened the Public Library, Borough Road, Southwark, in February, 1899, and instituted a comparison between living in London three or four centuries ago and the present time. Society in London in those days was highly organised and banded together by a thousand ties of necessity and social intercourse which had long since ceased to exist. Every parish had its co-operative life and spirit, and the mere record of their number of charities showed how strong a local feeling was possessed by the pious and benevolent. There were also guilds and the system of apprenticeship, which associated the man who throve in business with his own trade. We were now living in a new London, which by its growth had destroyed most of the old associations ; and if new ties and new opportunities of social intercourse and human sympathy were not formed, we should have a city undermined and full of danger. There was one mode of utilising means which was perfectly safe and easy, and that was by providing facilities for improvement and association which poor people could not provide for themselves, and among them were public libraries.

———

The *City Press*, on May 6th, 1899, gave an account of the ceremonial presentation of the Hon. Freedom of the Stationers' Company to Mr. Passmore Edwards. Sir Sydney Waterlow, the chief official who acted on the occasion, said to the large dinner party after the ceremony that, in acting as they did, the Stationers' Company were conferring an honour on themselves rather than upon the recipient, as Mr. Edwards had won a national reputation by his promotion of educational and charitable institutions. He had been a wise and generous benefactor to the printing and the allied trades. He built the Caxton Convalescent Home, provided a technical library in connection with St. Bride's Foundation, and was a large contributor to the Printers' Corporation. He had scattered his benefactions in the form of institutions over the country, and he (Sir Sydney) was proud of the fact that Mr. Edwards had accepted the Hon. Freedom of the Stationers' Company, as it was some recognition of the noble philanthropy which had characterised his life. A similar honour had been conferred on only four others, including the Right Hon. W. H. Smith, Sir John Evans, K.C.B., and Sir Edward Maude Thompson, K.C.B., Principal of the British Museum.

———

On June 23rd, 1899, the Duke and Duchess of York opened the Home for Epileptic Girls and also the Home for Epileptic Boys at Chalfont. The Duke of York, in his address, said it had been proved that an occupied and an active life was the best antidote to the deterioration, mental and moral, that usually accompanies epileptic patients, of whom there were computed to be 40,000 in the United Kingdom ; and it was intended by the society to give many of them opportunities denied them in ordinary life. When fully developed the colony would be an industrial village, whose inhabitants, though afflicted, would be usefully and helpfully occupied. The society had been attended by the happiest results. In the farm, garden, and workshops every member of the community had an opportunity of being engaged in some useful industry. The colonists played cricket matches with local teams, and considerable improvement had taken place in their condition, and particularly among the youngest members ; and all who had helped to maintain and administer the colony had the satisfaction of knowing that they contributed to a good and growing society which was much wanted, and which would in the future increase its claims to public recognition and support.

———

Lord Amherst, Pro-Grand Master of England and Provincial Grand Master of Kent, laid, with elaborate Masonic ceremony, the foundation-stone of the Railway Men's Convalescent Home, Herne Bay, in June, 1899. At the luncheon which followed, with Mr. J. E. Nichols in the chair, the Pro-Grand Master said, when he was invited to perform the ceremony he immediately consented to do so, as Brother Passmore Edwards had amassed a considerable fortune, and was now using it to promote the health and happiness of his fellow-men. He was much struck by a pamphlet he had just perused which contained illustrations and accounts of a large number of institutions founded by Brother Passmore Edwards in different parts of the country during Her Majesty's Diamond Jubilee, and the last and not least was the one they were commencing that day. As to the generous donor, they would say, in the words from the Book which was found in all their lodges : " He hath dispersed, he hath given to the poor, his righteousness endureth for ever ; his horn shall be exalted with honour."

———

When Principal Fairbairn, on Midsummer Day, 1899, declared the Boys' Club connected with the Mansfield House Settlement, Canning Town, opened, he said the boy was the father to the man ; it was impossible to make good men out of bad boys ; and boys were not made good by chance, but by honest labour and great patience. What was greatly wanted was to teach people to find more amusement in the ordinary course of life, and one of the objects of the Boys' Club was to help its members to find that amusement which would make them better men, and which could not be found in the streets of a town or the lanes of a village. What was wanted was to enlarge boys' views, and make them feel that they are both citizens of England and citizens of the world. True citizenship does not mean singing " Rule Britannia," which might be the mere expression of a spirit of brutal aggression or the opposite. It does not mean joining this or that political party, but giving oneself for the good of men, and being ready to serve the down-trodden and the poor ; and he hoped and believed that the Passmore Edwards Boys' Club and Institute they were commencing in Canning Town on that day would assist to build up good men, and thereby benefit the nation and mankind.

———

The Right Hon. Herbert Gladstone, M.P., opened the East Ham Public Library in September, 1899. He said the establishment of such a library would be a boon and blessing anywhere, and particularly in a district where the population was increasing by leaps and bounds. The conditions of modern life made it more and more difficult to cultivate systematic reading. They were living in the midst of certain conflicting tendencies. The hurry and racket of life seemed to be on the increase, and the tendency seemed to induce people not to sit down quietly, but to move about on some occupation or pleasure or activity which weakens the steady habitual taste for reading. Then there was the great spread of newspaper literature, and he hoped that nobody would think when he had read a newspaper for half an hour that he had done any serious reading. Instead of spending a quiet afternoon, there were now trains and trams to take them to all kinds of amusements. A well-supplied library in their midst would be an attraction for all, and an additional inducement to many to cultivate habits of reading. He felt that all connected with that district should make some acknowledgment to his friend Mr. Passmore Edwards, for his munificence, first in supplying a public library to afford recreation to the mind, and then for building a hospital close by to supply restoration for the body.

———

The Willesden Hospital was so much wanted that, within six years of the time it was opened in 1893 by the Right Hon. A. J. Balfour and his sister, it had to be enlarged from nine to twenty-three beds. The enlargement was opened in May, 1899, by Lady Campbell-Bannerman, and Sir Henry Campbell-Bannerman, in reply to a vote of thanks, said the ceremony that day carried with it two remarkable developments—one was the generous conduct of Mr. Passmore Edwards, who appeared to be going about doing nothing else than to search for fresh opportunities of employing his means for the benefit of the health, the recreation, and the elevation of his fellow-men ; and the other was that a very large proportion of the money subscribed for the maintenance of the Hospital came, not from the exuberance of the wealthy, but in small subscriptions from less well-to-do people. The increase of the population of London was traceable to the constant migration from the country to the town of men seeking for better-paid employment or for a larger horizon of life.

The tendency to congregate in great towns existed in every civilised country; and the increase of the suburbs of London was largely caused by the anxiety of working men to find healthful homes, at a moderate charge, in decent conditions of existence. It was a serious question for all, whether philosophers or economists, philanthropists or politicians. It was a positive danger to the country that those who, by their labour, were building up its prosperity, were compelled to live in houses and amid surroundings inconsistent with the comforts and decencies of life.

The Cornwall Central Technical Schools, at Truro, were opened by Lord Mount Edgcumbe, Lord-Lieutenant of the county, in October, 1899. At the banquet which followed, Sir George Smith, in proposing the health of the founder, said: "The benefactor who brings the skilled brain into harmony with the horny hand, the benefactor who, instead of causing the workman to be discontented with his task, causes him to be proud of it and interested in it, is a benefactor whom England should honour. The time is come when, while preserving physical manhood, we must, for national safety and social good, link brain and hand; we must take a pride in the artisan's work; we must make it interesting for him by the exercise and development of his intellect. It is on these grounds that I rejoice with you at the erection of this magnificent pile of buildings, for a no less magnificent purpose, and I call upon you to drink to the health of the founder, Mr. Passmore Edwards."

When Lady Tweedmouth, in July, 1900, laid the foundation-stone of the East Ham Hospital, Lord Tweedmouth, who accompanied her, and who spoke in her name, made particular reference to the rapid growth of the district, which had increased from 1,500 to 100,000 in half a century. He also said that Mr. Passmore Edwards travelled from east to west, and from north to south, and, whenever he put his foot down and looked well around, some institution for the benefit of the people was pretty sure to spring up. Scores of such institutions, representing almost every side or phase of educational and philanthropic activity, owed their existence to his persistent generosity. He first provided for the mental needs of the people of East Ham, and was now as generously providing for their physical needs.

The West Ham Museum and Institute was opened in October, 1900, by Lady Warwick, who said the new institution would become the permanent home for the collections of the Essex Field Clubs, which had been accumulating collections for twenty years. A local museum could alone meet the requirements of the present age. The association of a county museum with the Technical Institute adjoining was an alliance which would prove essentially helpful to both, and the educational advantages would be manifold and valuable. Mr. Passmore Edwards, with his splendid public spirit, might feel assured that his provision of the museum building would prove fruitful to future generations, while the naturalists might now go to work with redoubled industry, in order to fill the cabinets with collections worthy of the institution, the county, and the club.

———

Sir Henry Campbell-Bannerman opened the new Convalescent Home for Railway Men, at Herne Bay, on June 8th, 1901. Two special trains, taking more than 1,000 passengers, left London to attend the ceremony. Sir Henry Campbell-Bannerman said he had known Mr. Passmore Edwards for many years. He had known him as a respected and useful member of Parliament, and as one who had abandoned that career. He relinquished the charm of listening to tiresome speeches from other people and the still greater charm of making tiring speeches himself. All that he had renounced, and for many years had devoted himself to finding out, in various parts of the country, different philanthropic objects on which he not only expended his money, but upon which he bestowed his personal care in seeing that the money was well expended. The Railway Men's Convalescent Home was an instance of his assiduity in the new life which he had taken to follow. That Home was much wanted. No less than 15,581 men were injured annually at their work, many of whom would in the future reap convalescent benefit from the institution they were then dedicating to public use.

———

The Duke of Fife and Lord Mayor Green placed in position the memorial-stones of the Sailors' Palace, Limehouse, July, 1901. The Duke said it was a source of sincere gratification to him that the Sailors' Palace would ever be associated with the name of Passmore Edwards. In it the returning sailor would find a home in every sense of the word— a place of rest, recreation, and enjoyment—a haven of refuge from the perils and dangers of the shore, which were often more dangerous than those of the winds and the waves. The sailor was not now, as formerly, allowed to drift about like a ship without a rudder, unwatched and uncared-for.

The Bishop of Hereford presented an address to the Duke of Fife, and said that the stone that day was laid in hope and love, and in the belief that the society which had done so much for sailors for nearly a century would do much more in the future. The Sailors' Palace would illustrate in some measure the great conception embodied in the society's title—that sailors of all nations, irrespective of creed, colour, or country, shall find within its portals a warm welcome and friendly shelter.

The Prince of Wales, accompanied by the Princess of Wales, opened the Sailors' Palace in May, 1903. The Prince said the British and Foreign Sailors' Society ought to be grateful to the many Ambassadors, Ministers, and other foreign representatives who had honoured it with their presence on the occasion of celebrating the opening of such a splendid building, which had been principally erected through the liberality of Mr. Passmore Edwards. The Society was further indebted to him for the gift of 5,000 standard volumes to the Passmore Edwards

Ocean Library. Eighty-five years ago the Society began its work in London, and since then had extended its operations to all parts of the world, and Sailors' Rests and Institutions had been established in about 100 different ports. The Society endeavoured to make the merchant sailor realise that his future must depend upon himself, his personal character, and self-control. Recognising his difficulties, his weaknesses, and his temptations, the Society threw open its doors to him, welcomed him with sympathy and brotherly attention, and offered him, in the ports where it had stations, a home where thrift and temperance were encouraged, and where he was protected from dangers to which he was still exposed. He was glad to know that there was also established within the walls of the institution a nautical school, which would bear the name of King Edward VII. The object was to help our merchant seamen in their studies, and would, no doubt, be successful in advancing the general welfare of our mercantile marine.

Mr. Choate, the American Ambassador, in moving a vote of thanks to the Prince and Princess, said all nations were gathered there to do honour to the occasion, literally from China to Peru ; and they all congratulated Mr. Passmore Edwards on the rare opportunity which was given to him of enjoying his own immortality, his own posthumous fame ; for what all England was saying about him now was what posterity would say about him for many generations.

Lord Kimberley took the chair when Dr. Creighton, Bishop of London, placed in position the memorial-stone of University Hall, Clare Market. The Chairman said it would be difficult to estimate the importance and value of the London School of Economics and Political Science, which would find a permanent home in the new building about to be provided, and for which they would be indebted to Mr. Passmore Edwards, who had shown so great a desire to multiply and improve the facilities for scientific education. He (the Chairman) had been furnished with a list of the subjects taught, and to be taught, in the School ; he was astonished at their number, variety, and value, and they appeared to embrace a large portion of the knowledge of the world. The time would come when it would be necessary for anyone who desired to become a Minister of State, or public functionary, to undergo a successful examination in most of the subjects included in their curriculum.

The Right Hon. H. H. Asquith laid the foundation-stone of the Plaistow Library in October, 1902. He said he was more than glad to be able to show any mark, however slight, of acknowledgment and gratitude for the splendid and long-continued service rendered to the State by his friend Mr. Passmore Edwards, who had done more than any single living Englishman to help the people to equip and educate themselves for civic and social duty. The monuments of his enlightened munificence were found in every part of the country. The institutions, of one kind or another, for which he was responsible, numbered over seventy, and no fewer than fourteen of them were to be found in the East of London.

That was a remarkable record, and he was not using the language of flattery when he predicted that generation after generation of students would hold his name in honour and in gratitude for opening to them the very gateway of knowledge ; and, in countless cases, for giving facilities which they would not otherwise have enjoyed in the most insatiable of all pursuits—the reading of books. It was quite possible that there was in the literary production of the present day an excessive proportion of that which was trivial and ephemeral. It was also true that there would always be found among the frequenters of public libraries a considerable number of persons who went there to browse upon the lightest fare ; but the broad fact remained that libraries, such as that then founded, offered not only facilities and opportunities, but he might say inducements and temptations to self-culture, which could not otherwise be provided, and which were of incalculable value to the character and capacity of the British nation.

Mr. Andrew Carnegie, the great library-builder, opened the Plaistow Library in May, 1903. He said he found himself for the first time in the delightful position of opening a public library to which he had not contributed a penny. The real advantage of wealth was that it enabled its possessor to benefit his fellows. Mr. Passmore Edwards was a man who spent little upon himself, and was the liver of a quiet, unostentatious, and inexpensive life, disdaining luxury, and religiously devoting his entire surplus for the good of man—a form of worship which Franklin had pronounced the most acceptable. Mr. Edwards was a leading and true disciple of the gospel of wealth, which holds the duty of the rich to be to live simply, to scorn delights and live laborious days, in the service of their fellow-men. He had known him for many years as a man of extraordinary character, and a century in advance of his time ; one who will be regarded by future generations as a true benefactor of his race, and as one who would stand against a majority of his countrymen in denouncing a popular war or any measure he considered wrong. He would call him "Saint Passmore," and had he lived a hundred years before he would have been canonised. Mr. Carnegie, in referring to the Library, said the Shakespeares and the Bacons, the great writers and the great inventors, were from the ranks of the working classes, and workers in coming to the Plaistow Library should look upon it as their property and their home. He opened that temple in the faith that it would never prove anything but a fountain from which blessed water would ever flow.

————

Sir Wm. Broadbent laid the corner-stone of the Central Administrative Block at Chalfont St. Peters in June, 1903. After enlarging on the notable and characteristic work done by the National Society for the Employment of Epileptics, he expressed his appreciation of the assistance rendered to the colony by Mr. Passmore Edwards, who, after purchasing the land, provided for the use of the colonists five suitable buildings besides the one then commenced. The next century would find the country dotted over with institutions named after him, and used in one way or another for the real and permanent good of the community. It was well known that whatever he took up, it was not merely a charity which appealed to the heart, but one which the intellect justified; and the point which characterised him was that his munificence was expended not for the gratification of feeling, but for the advancement of his fellow-men, and this was particularly seen in his cordial co-operation with their Society for the benefit of epileptics.

Lady Carrington, accompanied by Lord Carrington, fixed the memorial stone of the Camberwell Polytechnic in July, 1903. Dr. Macnamara, M.P., in supporting a vote of thanks, said they had recently heard a great deal about the future of the British Empire; but it was not the people who talked the most who did the most or the best for the Empire. He considered that the future strength and stability of the Empire would principally depend on the physical, intellectual, and moral equipment of its individual units; and the providers of public libraries and polytechnic institutions, similar to the one they were then commencing in Camberwell, were builders and strengtheners of the Empire in the best sense of the words. There was not a report from a British Consul in the United States or Germany which did not say that the great commercial success of these countries was due to a sound, broad-based, and firmly-founded system of popular education, upon which had been raised superstructures of technical education.

Lord Ebrington, Lord-Lieutenant of Devon, opened in September, 1904, the Newton Abbot Public Library, and said he was deputed, on behalf of the people of the district, to thank Mr. Passmore Edwards for his generous gift. He (the speaker) said his ideal, beyond the one of trying to do his duty, was the maintenance of the British Empire. It had been the fashion on public occasions for some time past to emphasise and extol the Empire; but, after all, ours was not the only Empire that had been great. Ever since the days of Babylon, one after another, empires had waxed and waned, and there was no more deserving study for those who intended to use the library than the study of the causes which led to the disruption and decay, one after another, of the great nations which in succession held a leading place in the world. It was only by studying those causes they could hope to postpone or prevent what had hitherto seemed the inevitable fate of every great nation. He, therefore, hoped that those who used the library might devote themselves to historical study, as there was nothing more worthy of the attention of all lovers of their country or more calculated to stimulate their higher patriotism, which looked beyond the questions of the day, than the ultimate interests of the Empire, which we hoped our sons would hand on unimpaired to their descendants.

The *Times* of November 1st, 1900, said: " The London Society for the Extension of University Teaching is making an interesting experiment.

The Council of the Society approached Mr. Passmore Edwards, and asked him to endow six courses of lectures on Modern English History, to be given by well-known University Extension lecturers at free libraries in London. This he consented to do, bearing the whole cost of the lectures, so that no charge be made for admission. The experiment is being attended with remarkable success. Each course consists of ten lectures. In some cases many were unable to obtain admission, the halls being full before the commencement of the lectures. The librarian in each centre has acted as secretary for the course, and has entered into the work with the greatest energy and enthusiasm."

The *Oxford Magazine* of May 1st, 1901, says : "The *Oxford Gazette* contains the announcement of a very interesting and generous benefaction in the offer by Mr. John Passmore Edwards of a Scholarship for the encouragement of the study of English Literature in its connection with the Classical Literatures of Greece and Rome. His name is already associated with libraries and settlements. His liberality and his desire to encourage things of the kind are well known, but it comes as an agreeable surprise that he should become a 'benefactor' of one of the old Universities. His name, however, will now deservedly take its place in the long series of those we commemorate, and his foundation bids fair to be one of the most interesting of such endowments."

WATTS AND CO.'S
SIXPENNY PUBLICATIONS.

HUXLEY'S LECTURES AND ESSAYS. (A Selection.) With Autobiography.

MODERN SCIENCE AND MODERN THOUGHT. By SAMUEL LAING. With Illustrations.

*LITERATURE AND DOGMA. By MATTHEW ARNOLD.

*EDUCATION: Intellectual, Moral, and Physical. By HERBERT SPENCER.

HUMAN ORIGINS. By SAMUEL LAING.

TYNDALL'S LECTURES AND ESSAYS. (A Selection.) With Biographical Sketch.

THE ORIGIN OF SPECIES. By CHARLES DARWIN.

EMERSON'S ADDRESSES & ESSAYS.

ON LIBERTY. By JOHN STUART MILL.

*THE STORY OF CREATION. By EDWARD CLODD.

LIFE OF JESUS. By ERNEST RENAN.

A MODERN ZOROASTRIAN. By SAMUEL LAING.

THREE ESSAYS ON RELIGION. By JOHN STUART MILL.

THE APOSTLES. By ERNEST RENAN.

PROBLEMS OF THE FUTURE. By S. LAING.

*GOD AND THE BIBLE. By MATTHEW ARNOLD.

THE CHILDREN'S BOOK OF MORAL LESSONS. By F. J. GOULD. First Series.

THE FUTURE PEACE OF THE ANGLO-SAXONS. By Major STEWART L. MURRAY. With Preface by Field-Marshal EARL ROBERTS, K.G.

The whole of the above list, with the exception of those marked with an asterisk, are supplied in cloth at 1s.

The postage on a single copy is 2d. (paper covers) or 3d. (cloth); but five or more will be sent carriage paid, at the published price, to any address in the United Kingdom.

WATTS & CO.,
17, JOHNSON'S COURT, FLEET STREET, LONDON, E.C.

PRINTED BY WATTS AND CO., 17, JOHNSON'S COURT, FLEET STREET, LONDON, E.C.

9 781535 800181